GOOSE CHASE

Capturing the Energy of Change in Logistics

JIM TOMPKINS
with
Brenda Jernigan

Tompkins Press
Raleigh, North Carolina

For information, address: Tompkins Press
2809 Millbrook Road
Raleigh, NC 27616

First Printing: August 1997
Printed in the United States of America

Library of CongressCataloging-in-Publication Data

Tompkins, Jim
Goose chase / Jim Tompkins
97-90628
ISBN 0-9658659-0-8

— Dedication —

We dedicate this book to all the people who are focused on moving their organizations to the next level of performance. We dedicate this book to all clients of Tompkins Associates with much gratitude for their confidence in our ability to produce results. We dedicate this book to all people in leadership positions who, much like Rich, are daily fighting the goose chase.

Most of all we dedicate this book to our families who have endured our "goose chase" as we have allocated time to this book that could have been allocated to them.

Thank you.

JT

BJ

GOOSE CHASE

Capturing the Energy of Change in Logistics

"Change is just another word for the latest management goose chase."

— Mark Perkins, during a conversation at the Ram's Head Bar with his co-worker, Mike Fulton, January

CHAPTER ONE

Bob Ketchum waved the women's camisoles above his head like one of Custer's men trying to surrender.

"You want to know why I'm over my budget? I'll tell you. It's like this. Marcus Warren and those maniacs over in purchasing go out and get themselves great deals on these camisole things. Nobody ever mentions that part of the reason they are such great deals is because they come in here without thinking about us needing to provide customers with floor-ready merchandise."

Bob shook one of the white plastic hangers at Rich Morrison. The attached camisole danced like a marionette.

"I'm talking the size my ten-year-old granddaughter would wear packed in the same carton as the size my mother-in-law could use. And my mother-in-law passed huge a decade ago. Guess what? The box only has one label. So we've got to go into the box and pull the things out and figure what the hell size they are and then try to get those skinny straps on hangers, add our labels, repackage them and then hold them until our orders come in. This month it's these camisole things, next month, who knows—"

"I understand." Rich held up his hand. "But the Rollins store chain is going to start imposing significant penalties on us if we don't comply with their labeling requirements. And Marcus Warren doesn't care if you are over budget, but Donald Stabler sure will."

Donald Stabler was the CEO of Stabler Consolidated, a lingerie and accessories manufacturer. About a year ago Stabler purchased Kinton Lingerie, Inc., the company that Rich and Bob worked for in Charlotte, North Carolina.

Bob retained his position as head of the Charlotte distribution center, but Rich was another story. When Stabler bought Kinton, Rich was the vice president of marketing for Kinton; a month later he was distribution manager for Stabler Consolidated.

It happened that fast. Rich replaced the former distribution manager for Kinton who took early retirement after the buyout. One day Rich was complaining about distribution problems; the next he was heading up the department. Before he knew what was happening, he was head of logistics for Stabler reporting to the vice president of operations.

He had been putting out fires ever since, hardly knowing whether he was coming or going, working like a crazy man. That was before Donald Stabler went on a tear buying up any company that had ever thought of being in the lingerie business. And then there was Walter, his son. Donald Stabler was a pain-in-the-ass with vision; Walter was simply a pain-in-the-ass with power. Walter was the vice president of operations for Stabler; manufacturing, planning and logistics reported to him. He would fly in often enough to get every one of Rich's people working on trying to fit a square peg into a round hole and then he was gone again, flying off to make someone else's life hell.

Bob thumped the desk one more time for emphasis. "I'm telling you this is crazier than hell. It is killing morale."

Rich agreed. "I know it's crazy. But it's like this, Bob—Donald Stabler is so busy out buying that he won't ever notice the budget overruns, but Walter will be happy to point it out to him. Anything to try and win himself some points with the old man. Walter's got a productivity timeline to meet, you know." Walter always had a timeline neatly laid out for his latest fetish.

"Well, you know what he can do with his timeline. All this hot air about a productivity timeline, it's just like when he came in here pushing that team stuff down our throats. Next week it will be some other fad that he thinks is exciting."

"Not all of his ideas are so bad, Bob. It's how they are implemented that's the problem," Rich said.

Walter used the stuff he read in books and heard at conferences like a meat cleaver instead of a surgeon's scalpel. What was it Mark Twain said? There's a whole lot of difference between lightning and a lightning bug, something like

2

that. With someone like Bob Ketchum there was no need to mince words or work fancy gimmicks, but still there was some finesse that Walter seemed to lack. Bob was a meat-and-potatoes sort of fellow. Walter got that part right, he just served the meat raw. Before Walter ever opened his mouth, Bob's blood pressure went up at least twenty points.

Bob continued. "It is just like my sister-in-law back when she read that Dr. Spock book and tried to raise her kids that way. It was crazy. The kids are lucky to be alive. One's in the big house in Joliet, and the other's a priest."

"Look, Bob, I know Walter can be difficult, but he's not going to go anywhere. So we can figure out how to work around him or we can quit. Standing still is not an option."

"If Walter keeps helping us out, quitting won't be an option. We'll be out of business. Forty years of my life down the toilet cause some kid is playing vice president. Quitting is better than watching this company get run into the ground. My health is going right along with it. I buy Maalox by the case."

Rich reached up and rubbed his neck, trying to work out a kink that had become a recurring problem directly tied to Walter's name.

"So do you want to be a notch in Walter's briefcase handle or are you going to help me figure out how to get out of this hole that's been dug so nicely for us?"

Rich hoped he sounded more optimistic than he felt. Bob's face was starting to take on a gray-green color. The last thing they needed was for Bob to land in the hospital. It wasn't worth that high a price, for Bob or Rich or anyone.

Bob sometimes got caught up in the "We've always done it that way" mentality. Despite that, Rich thought he had real possibility to be a part of taking the next step Stabler needed to be a world-class distribution operation.

"I don't know, Rich. You get to the point, where you ask yourself, is this really worth it? And what do you know? You're a marketing guru that got thrown into the distribution cesspool. You're just trying to get back out without a permanent stink attached to you. This warehouse is my life."

Before Rich could reply, Bob's intercom buzzed and his secretary, Darla, announced, "Security wants you to know that there are pickets all out across the front of the building. It looks like the news crews are setting up their cameras to record for this evening's news."

"What have we done to be on the evening news?" Bob asked.

"It could be that Rita Sue Fox is leading the group of pickets." Darla's tone was sarcastic.

Rita Sue Fox was an actress who had parlayed her television stardom into endorsement contracts and clothing lines, only to discover that her lingerie line was produced in sweatshops in Indonesia. This led to her latest crusade to stop all imports produced in conditions that did not meet her standards.

"That's all we need," Rich said. "Her out front causing a ruckus about her factory standards." Both men headed for the door.

Darla announced, "Rich, Marcus Warren is holding on line two for you."

"Tell him I'll call him back," Rich told her as he went past her desk.

They heard the noise of the pickets before they saw them. A line of people had blocked the entrance to the access road and circled the pavement shouting, "Every Child Counts!" They carried placards that read, 'Stabler Exploits Kids' and 'Third World Children Deserve a Childhood Too.'

"So what the hell do they think—that we don't care about kids?" Bob muttered.

The group's activity increased as the cameraman swung his camera in their direction. From the center of the crowd emerged Rita Sue Fox. Rita Sue's long blonde hair fanned out around her as she clacked toward Rich and Bob in high heels and a dress that in a different shade could have passed for a second skin. Behind her followed a woman in a blue suit with a skirt that barely made it past the hem of her jacket and a young guy with a ponytail dressed in jeans, T-shirt and a leather jacket. Even with the jacket covering his arms, his muscles were noticeable.

The kink in Rich's neck got worse as he tried to remember the last time he'd worked out. Unconsciously he sucked his stomach in before he spoke.

"Ms. Fox, I'm Rich Morrison with Stabler Consolidated. Is there something I can help you with?"

A woman with a helmet of petrified blonde hair made a beeline for the group, dragging a microphone and a cameraman with her.

"Donna Daytona, Channel 7 News. Ms. Fox, what can you tell us about your demonstration today?" Her words were clipped, and she had an attitude that said 'Walk softly, but carry a big microphone.'

"Ms. Fox will be happy to answer your questions in a few minutes."

Rich spoke to the reporter giving her a look that he hoped said, 'back off,' as he took Rita's elbow and guided her away from the cameras and toward the distribution center's entrance. "Why don't we step inside where we can talk without so many people around?" Rita's two assistants followed in her wake. The woman, whom Rita referred to as Bev, made copious notes on her clipboard as they walked.

Rich heard Donna Daytona utter an unprofessional oath. It was the first time he had seen Bob Ketchum smile all day.

"Score one for the good guys."

Rita drew back her elbow but continued to walk beside Rich. "I'm glad someone is finally willing to talk. I've called Mr. Stabler's office all week and couldn't get an answer to my questions." She smiled sweetly, turning the full wattage of her smile onto Rich. "So while it is true that you catch more flies with honey, you've also got to know when to take the offensive. Without being offensive, of course."

Rich smiled back at her. "I'm sure you could never offend anyone, Ms. Fox. Which Mr. Stabler's office did you call?"

"Please call me Rita." She turned to the suited woman. "Bev, what was that man's name?

Bev consulted her clipboard. "Walter."

"The last time I called I told them exactly what I was going to do, but I still couldn't get anybody to return my calls."

So Walter knew this was coming, Rich cursed silently. Wait until he got the little milquetoast on the phone.

"I'm sorry to hear that, but why don't we go inside? I feel sure we can resolve this situation to everyone's satisfaction."

Even as Bob opened the door to the lobby, the crowd that had been watching through the window scattered, leaving Darla to stand alone at the window checking her watch as if she were waiting for a late date.

"Darla, why don't you show our guests to the conference area off Mr. Ketchum's office. I need to make one quick call." Rich motioned toward the conference area and then circled around to find an empty office where he could talk privately.

Rich's wife, Melissa, ran her own advertising agency. Public relations was not really her niche, but for a few select clients, and her husband, she made exceptions. Rich tried to remember back to breakfast that morning. Had she said anything like, "Don't forget I'll be in outer Mongolia all day?" Nothing came readily to mind. Since he started this logistics project, Melissa had accused him of not really listening and would occasionally test him by saying, "What did I just say?" He'd gotten pretty good at repeating back her last sentence, but the bottom line was she was right—he wasn't listening.

As he waited for Melissa to get on the line, he silently fumed over Walter's behavior. *The man has a major PR issue on his hands, a demonstration at one of my DCs and he can't even be bothered to call me. If office supplies in the Fulton County DC had gone up a thousand bucks last year, he'd have had me on the phone before the financials were out of the printer.*

Rich got his first break of a very long day. Melissa was in and once she quit laughing, she listened carefully and dispensed her advice on how to hold off the barbarians at the gate or, in this case, the pickets on the sidewalk. She could not resist a final verbal nudge.

"And how do you intend to pay for this expert consulting, Mr. Morrison?"

"How about we take it out in trade?"

"I think I'm too tired for that. How about you bring Chinese home for supper, and we'll call it even."

"I'll have to take a raincheck on that. I'm sure I'll be later than you and the kids want to eat."

"Have I ever told you the story of the guy who worked so much that his family left him and he ended up a bum on Skid Row?"

"Not likely."

"Okay, okay. He ended up with a BMW convertible and an in-car fax machine, but it was a totally useless existence. See you tonight."

Rich's next call was to Kurt Thomas, head of Stabler corporate communications. Rich advised him of what had been done and arranged for him to set up a meeting between him and Rita Sue's people.

As Rich walked into the conference room, he heard Rita Sue giggle like a school girl at something Bob Ketchum had said. Her two assistants laughed politely with a 'the boss is laughing, better laugh' variety. Bob motioned toward Rich.

"Ask Rich, if you don't believe me. Rich, isn't it true that after Rita Sue wore that red bustier thing to the Oscars that we had three buyers out scouting for red lace for months?"

"He's right. One of our buyers had just gotten a great deal on black lace for bustiers. They were the hottest thing going. After Oscar night we couldn't give the things away. Every store we deal with was screaming for red."

Rich set up the meeting between Rita Sue and Kurt Thomas's group. Meanwhile she explained that all she needed for Stabler to do was investigate fully every vendor they dealt with to assure her that children all over the world were having a proper childhood.

Rich nodded intently, not bothering to tell her that he wasn't even sure what warehouse and distribution operations they owned from day to day, let alone who they had manufacturing products for them. Sounded damn near impossible to Rich, so he took the course of least resistance and fudged. He told her the home office had assured him they were going to look into it. And he reminded her that her corporate contact would be Kurt Thomas in corporate communications. He even spelled Kurt's name for the ever-scribbling Bev. Rich prayed that Kurt would be able to satisfy Rita or that the next movie she shot would be close to corporate headquarters. Hey, no guts, no glory.

Rita bounced off with Bev and Mr. Muscles in her wake. Rich went back in the building and closed the conference room door. It was time for a little talk with Walter.

"Change? You know what my ex-wife said to me about change. 'I'd rather go to hell and talk with the devil hisself than to try to talk you into anything new.'"

— Wayne Hicks to his buddies from the Stabler plant while on a fishing trip to the coast, February

CHAPTER TWO

"I'm up to my a-double-s in alligators here." Walter Stabler had a whine to his voice that set people's teeth on edge. "I can't return every phone call that comes through this office."

It quickly became apparent to Rich that Walter was going to be no help at all, nor was he going to own up to his contribution to the Rita Sue disaster. He did, however, have a piece of advice for Rich.

"You might want to try and get a handle on these new warehouses that Donald's acquiring. These penalties that the Rollins chain are talking about have him torn up. He told me just yesterday that he has his doubts about your distribution talents."

Rich kicked at the leg of the conference room table. "So what are you saying, Walter? Is he going to can me, or simply transfer me to Alaska?"

"All I'm saying, Rich, is that the distribution network better show some kind of progress or Donald may just outsource the whole thing."

Rich refrained from saying his first thought on the subject of outsourcing. Idle threats.

"Look, Walter, we've got cross-functional issues impacting our distribution network. Bob Ketchum was just telling me how the buyers' great deals are eating up his warehouse budget. He's having to meet more rigorous customer standards and do more product customization, but the goods are arriving at the DC in worse and worse shape. All the sizes together in the cartons. Conformance to standards is a foreign language to our manufacturers."

"I understand your problem. Really, Rich, you've got my sympathy. I'm just the messenger. But between you and me, Donald got a call yesterday from Howie Whitehead. Whitehead's thinking about canceling the contract they gave us because some outfit went in and pitched how they could comply to all labeling standards and ticket their product differently for all 300 stores for cheaper than we're meeting their present requirements. You know how far back Dad and Howie go."

Every now and then Walter slipped and referred to the elder Stabler as Dad. Rich knew how far back Donald and Howie went—back to the days when Stabler was a simple men's underwear baron, his motto similar to that of Henry Ford's: "Any color of briefs or boxers you want as long as it is white." Rich kicked the table leg again. Now Stabler was the king of all intimate apparel and Rich was about to be beheaded over a problem he hadn't even known existed. Wasn't Marcus Warren in charge of the Whitehead account? Rich could not help wondering why Marcus hadn't mentioned the problem. It wasn't like him to run from a customer service issue. Rich made himself a note to check with Marcus on that.

Walter continued, "What happened to those teams we implemented? I thought we would be winning awards by now."

Rich wondered if he had kept the phone number of the headhunter who had called him last week.

"Walter—"

"Maybe what we need is more training. I'll have Lisa call that woman in charge of your personnel department. What was her name again?"

"Valerie Wagner. Walter, I'll check on the Whitehead account and get back to you. Meanwhile, if any more starlets call your office have them call Kurt Thomas. He's casting our latest Stabler movie, 'Crocodile Undie.'"

"Good one, Rich. It's good to see you haven't lost your sense of humor."

Before he left the building, Rich stopped back by Bob Ketchum's office, hoping to talk with him about the Whitehead account and get a commitment from him for some sort of understanding of their need to change.

"Have you heard of any problems we're having with the Whitehead account?"

Bob shrugged. "They're like everyone else. They want us to do everything but hang product on their sales floor. Overall, I thought they were satisfied. Ask

Marcus Warren. It's my job to get it out of here right; it's his job to schmooze with the customers."

"That may be the case; however, we've got to look at improving our responsiveness. Walter tells me Howie Whitehead has been on the phone with Donald saying he can get a higher level of customization with shorter lead times than what we're doing. I'm going to talk with Donald myself, but I think it's time we came up with a plan. Something that will give us some time to straighten out the mess we're in without Walter's help."

Bob leaned back in his chair. "You said the magic words. Without Walter. I'm not against things changing, Rich. I'm against things changing on the whim of some pretty boy. Especially one that even the Good Witch of the North couldn't please."

"The way I see it, either I prove to Donald Stabler that I can handle this logistics thing, or I go find myself a job in a company where the CEO never had kids."

Bob shook his head vigorously. "Nope, bad idea. Count me in on the change thing."

"I'll let you know when we can get a meeting scheduled." He picked up his briefcase and headed for the door. "Why the sudden change of heart, Bob?"

"Two reasons—because my people can't keep working like this. We're at the limit and because," Bob grinned at Rich, "if you leave they'll just send some bigger candy-ass down here and then where will I be? My heart can't take another one of you MBAs."

Rich let Bob have the last word. Before he walked out of Bob's office, he was already onto his next conversation. Talking with Donald Stabler was like talking to a whirling dervish with a high IQ. Donald changed the subject, paced the floor and then just when his attention seemed completely dissipated, he would hone in on the one area of the presentation that the presenter knew the least about and get a hold of it, shaking it like a terrier with its first taste of blood. Rich thought if you looked close you could almost see his tail wag. Donald Stabler enjoyed the legend of his temper almost as much as he enjoyed acquiring new operations.

Donald's secretary promised to have him call as soon as possible. When he finally caught up with Rich, the conversation was brief.

"Donald, I think it's time we had a meeting about our distribution operations. We've got to have some way of integrating our new operations into our old. Our efficiency is slipping and so is our customer service."

"From what I see on my end, Rich, efficiency isn't slipping, it has taken a swan dive off the ten-meter board. And customer service? Hell, I'm surprised you'd even mention the concept the way we're performing."

Rich knew better than to try and justify poor performance to Donald when he was in this mood. "Exactly. So instead of spending my time fighting fires, I think we'd be better off to use some dynamite to get a firebreak. Walter told me that Howie Whitehead had called you."

"That's right. It didn't make me happy either. I think you're right about the meeting. I've had my secretary schedule all the divisional people to Boston on Thursday. You and Walter and I'll meet afterward, so plan on taking the late flight. She'll call you with the details. Anything else, Rich?"

Rich outlined Rita Sue's visit and the temporary resolution.

Donald blew loudly into the phone. "That won't be the last of her. I've known since the fifties that Hollywood is full of Commies."

Rich wasn't about to touch that subject, not even to point out the fall of the Soviet Union. On that note, the conversation ended and Rich packed his briefcase for the night.

The briefcase was a soft-shell, brown leather case that Melissa and the kids had given him for Christmas, retiring the one they had presented him with when he received his MBA from Duke eleven years ago. He certainly hadn't imagined then that he'd have a career in logistics. With the way things were going, he might end up back in marketing. If he did, he wanted it to be his choice and not someone else's.

Rich had come from a long line of marketers. His grandfather had hired teams of horses to carry samples of Corn Toasties to every family in the city of Chicago, increasing sales 300 percent a year for three years in a row. The cereal company paid part of his salary in stock, making him a fairly wealthy man for the time. However, his grandfather wasn't satisfied with that, so when the opportunity came to sell his stock to a New York banker, he sold quickly and invested in land. The cereal company went public the next month, the land went bust. His grandfather went through many of these cycles during his life.

Consequently, Rich's father was cautious about his money. He had been a senior engineer with a large textile firm in Greensboro, North Carolina. Rich grew up there and his parents still lived there. Rich liked to think he had gotten his ability to sell and market from his grandfather and his good judgment from his dad. He thought how each would respond to the problems he faced at Stabler. "Make a plan," his father told him. "Do the unexpected," his grandfather said.

What Rich wanted right now was a good meal and a hot shower. His brain felt like he'd been on one of those rides at Disney World, as if it could orbit around the room without him.

Rich turned off the light to the office and stood quietly for a moment wondering what Donald had planned for their meeting and thinking of the challenges ahead. The lights in the outer office were out. Barbara, Rich's secretary, had stuck her head in the office an hour earlier to say goodnight.

After a brief conversation with the security guard at the front desk, Rich walked through the almost empty front parking lot. He entered his own cocoon, his Suburban. Other guys went for sporty little cars, but Rich wanted something that gave him enough space to stretch his legs and his thoughts as he drove home. By the time he reached home every night, he had metamorphosed into someone who could at least walk and talk at the same time.

As Rich exited the parking lot, he turned on the radio.

"More in a moment on teenagers who are being blackmailed into prostitution," a voice announced from the dashboard.

Where was Rita Sue Fox when she was really needed, he thought, as he reached for the radio dial. He'd left too late to listen to his favorite program, the one that Jack Thompson hosted. If he didn't get caught late at the office, he could tune in on his ride home. On occasion, he had even called in on his cell phone with questions for Jack. Often the show dealt with issues he faced at work, and at other times the radio host focused on up-and-coming issues in the world of business.

Unfortunately, if Rich left the office too late, he heard the next program host, Micki, who always addressed off-the-wall topics. Rich pushed the radio's power button sending Micki and her blackmailed prostitutes off into someone else's universe. Why is it, he wondered, that all talk show hosts who have only one name seem to be a few french fries short of a Happy Meal?

Turning onto the highway, Rich thought back over Walter's remark about teams. The reality was that the teams were working well, but Walter lacked patience. He didn't understand what Rich had already learned. Teams took time. You didn't just put seven people in a room for two meetings and have a team. Teaming was not a quick fix, but a process, a way of doing business.

All teams go through five phases: Forming, which is the watch-and-listen phase. Storming, where team members begin to vocalize their anxiety. Norming, where teams truly become teams. Performing, where teams start to feel the benefits of synergy. Oil change, where teams get recharged for ongoing continuous improvement. Most of the Stabler teams were storming, a few forming and only one had made it to the norming phase.

It was too early to expect teaming results. Rich understood that. How was he going to get Walter to understand that? Not just that, really—Walter needed to understand everything about teams. If he could get Walter to see that teaming was a process not a program, it would be much easier to bring him on board. Rich felt like a ship's captain trying to inspire everyone to pull together. If he couldn't do that, he may as well christen the ship the Titanic. Driving down the highway with the last of the sun's rays warming the Suburban's interior, Rich was oblivious, as the fated ship's captain had been, to some of the peril that waited all around him.

At home, he would bump the next icy chunk.

GOOSE CHASE

"All of us go through changes as we get older. Your dad treats you that way because he hates to lose his little girl. He has trouble remembering that it's the car and not your tricycle that we're discussing."

— Melissa Morrison to her daughter, Kelly, after a fight over driving privileges, February

CHAPTER THREE

The black Viper parked in the Morrison's front circular driveway bore a vanity license tag JTS. It was parked beside Melissa's dark blue Volvo wagon. Trying to place the owner of the black car, Rich eased his white Suburban past the sports car's bumper and into the garage. Melissa had not mentioned anything to him about company.

When he opened the door from the garage to the kitchen, Melissa called to him from the living room, "Honey, we're in here."

He dropped his briefcase at the end of the kitchen counter. From the smell of things, someone had brought home dinner, the Chinese. In the living room, Melissa sat talking to a slick-haired guy in a tailored suit. She smiled when Rich walked in.

"You won't believe who is here."

What the hell is J. Thomas Sewell doing here? Rich thought, sucking his gut in for the second time that day.

"Good to see you, Rich." Thomas stood to shake Rich's hand.

"Thomas, good to see you." The only person I'd enjoy seeing more might be an IRS agent, Rich thought. And why was Melissa wearing that Mona Lisa smile? Rich made it a point to kiss his wife before he sat down on the end of the couch that Sewell had left open for him.

"I'm trying to talk this wife of yours into selling her agency to us and coming on board as a vice president. Sewell & Prather would love to have her back in our corner."

"I've told Thomas I'd have to think about it and talk with you."

Sewell & Prather was the agency that Melissa had begun working for ten years ago when Andrew went off to kindergarten. After five years, Melissa had come to the realization that not only was she not going to be able to work flexible hours, but unless she consistently put in sixty hours a week, she would never see the title of vice president behind her name. Her answer to that was to start her own agency. She worked hard, but she worked her own schedule. Bumps in the road taught them both lessons about what worked for the business and their family. Eventually, Melissa's blood, sweat and creativity had paid off. Her agency, AdWorks, now employed fifteen people full-time. Andrew, fifteen, and Kelly, seventeen, worked part-time at the agency on holidays and summer breaks.

Rich wondered what Sewell & Prather had offered.

"I'm not surprised. I would expect Sewell & Prather to recognize the potential for the niche that Melissa has carved for herself and AdWorks in the market."

"Absolutely. And from talking with Melissa, I think she seems ready to shed that all-consuming responsibility that running your own shop entails," Thomas said.

Rich glanced at Melissa. He didn't recall hearing her say that. And he wasn't sure he liked the tone that Thomas used on the word "shed."

The phone rang. One half-ring was all it was allowed before somewhere upstairs Kelly snatched it from its cradle. She yelled downstairs in an exasperated voice, "Dad. Phone."

Rich excused himself and picked up the phone up in the kitchen. He made a futile attempt to talk with the head of the Habitat for Humanity's steering committee at the same time he listened to the living room conversation. It proved impossible. He promised to return the call later and made his way back to the living room. Thomas Sewell was standing by the front door. He waved good-bye to Melissa and Rich, promising to call Melissa the next day. At his car he paused and said, "Rich, haven't seen you playing racquetball for a while. Call me and we'll play."

Rich waved. "Will do." Rich couldn't remember the last time he played racquetball. It seemed like another lifetime. And Sewell wasn't keeping in shape by writing ad copy. No Kodak moments in that game.

"So how was your day? I mean once you got rid of Rita Sue and company," Melissa said.

"It was like I was in the business equivalent of a Bruce Willis movie. Every time I turned around there was some new ticking bomb and I couldn't decide if I was supposed to cut the red or the green wire. At least by the end of his movies, Bruce gets to shoot all the people that made him mad."

"Was it really that bad?" Melissa put her arms around his waist.

"It didn't hit rock bottom until I got home and J. Thomas Sewell was sitting in my living room."

She laughed. "What you need is some good home cooking."

"It smells like Chinese to me," Rich said.

"That's right, and Mr. Chen says he cooks the egg rolls at home. 'Not to worry, Mrs. Morrison, I cook good dinner for you, he tells me.'" Melissa pressed her palms together and bowed.

Melissa poured Rich a glass of chardonnay while his supper heated in the microwave. "So what do you think about Sewell & Prather?"

"I guess the question is, what do you think? I didn't realize that you were tired of running a business."

"I think the boys at Sewell & Prather would like me to think that I am."

"Have they given you a number? I guess those are my two questions. Are you ready to go back to work for them and what's the number?" Rich asked.

"No definite number yet. As far as ready to go to work for them, I could sell and get out," Melissa said.

"I must have had a harder day than I thought. I could have sworn you said you could get out." Rich rubbed his forehead as he spoke.

"I did."

"Is this the same woman who hissed ancient Malaysian curses on me if I mentioned that possibility?" Rich asked.

"But I've proven I can do it now. Maybe I'm ready for something completely different," Melissa said.

"Okay. So what would—"

A scream sounded in the upstairs hall and proceeded toward them in the kitchen, accompanied by the loud thumping of footsteps on the stairs. Kelly burst into the kitchen propelled by the force of the noise.

"Daddy, how could you? How could you?"

At seventeen, Kelly Morrison stood 5'10" and had thick auburn hair. Frequently, it was fixed as she wore it now, in a ponytail hanging out of a ball cap. Today's team was the Chicago Bulls.

She threw her hands in the air with all the melodrama of a silent movie actress. No captions were necessary. "I mean, Daddy, really, how could you?"

"Nice to see you too, Kelly. How could I what?"

"The evening news, all those poor children. They showed where they were being forced to work. How can you work for a company that takes advantage of little children?"

"Wait a minute. I haven't even seen the news. Did they show you these children?"

"Yes."

"And did they specifically say that the children they showed you worked for Stabler?"

"Yes." Kelly threw her hands in the air again. "Well, I don't know."

"It seems to me that we ought to tape the story at eleven. Then we can review it to see what they are actually saying about Stabler."

Kelly started shaking her head. "But Rita Sue Fox says—"

Rich interrupted. "I talked to Rita Sue Fox today. She doesn't have her facts straight, either. Before you go off into space, let's get the facts."

"That's fine with me, Daddy. But what are you going to do when you find out that your company exploits little children?"

Rich shrugged. "I'm going to sign you up for work-study. What do you expect me to do?"

Kelly let out a screech.

Melissa gave the time-out signal. "Kelly, your dad's right. Let's watch it first and then see what we think. No need to go off the deep end. Your dad hasn't even had his supper. We at least owe him that before we start trying to avenge the third world. No more serious discussion until he's eaten and had a chance to catch his breath."

Kelly sat down across the table from her father. "That's cool. Dad, did you see that car Thomas was driving? It was pure butter."

Rich nodded.

"He's not so bad either, a regular dime."

Rich didn't understand the last reference, but Kelly's opinion was apparent enough.

"I don't care if he's a quarter or a half-dollar, he's Mr. Sewell to you." Melissa echoed his sentiments. "No more 'Thomas' to you, young lady."

"Oh, pah-leez, you two. The man told me to call him Thomas while we were waiting for you to come downstairs, Mom."

"The man doesn't pay the bills here. And even though he's old enough to be your father, he is not making the rules. His name is Mr. Sewell. Now you say, 'Certainly Dad, anything you say.'" Rich pointed a fork in her direction.

Kelly rolled her eyes.

"Where's Andrew?" Rich asked.

Melissa made a face. "I guess you forgot you promised him you'd go to the Y and shoot hoops with him. He left after we ate, and since it's a school night, he should be home any minute."

Rich covered his face with his hands. "I completely forgot. He should have called."

"He did. You were on the phone with Mr. Stabler, so he told Barbara he'd talk to you when you got home."

Andrew came in about fifteen minutes later as Rich was finishing his supper. Andrew had his father's height. At fifteen, he was close to six feet tall with brown hair that he kept cut short during basketball season.

"Hey, Dad, what's up?" Andrew went to the refrigerator and poured himself a big glass of milk.

"I can't believe I forgot about the Y. Maybe we can make up for it this weekend. What do you think?"

"That's cool. Hey, guess what? Ninety percent of my post moves tonight—in the hole. Course my perimeter shots were in the basement." Andrew put his empty glass in the sink and raised his hand for a high five. Rich slapped his hand across Andrew's as he headed for the shower.

Alone in the kitchen, Rich had no idea how he was going to find time this weekend to play basketball with his son.

Rich turned the shower spray on full blast to work out the kink in his neck. He had made the mistake of falling asleep in his favorite chair while watching the Hornets/Knicks game. By the time he got out of the shower, the lights were out in the bedroom.

Melissa rolled toward him for a good-night kiss.

"You never said what you wanted to do if you don't go to work for Sewell & Prather."

Melissa kissed him on the lobe of his ear. "I want to have another baby."

GOOSE CHASE

"We trained hard, but it seemed that every time we were beginning to form up into teams, we would be reorganized. I was to learn later in life that we tend to meet any new situation by reorganizing; and a wonderful method it can be for creating the illusion of progress while producing confusion, inefficiency and demoralization."

— Petronius Arbiter, 210 B.C.
- Posted on the Stabler cafeteria bulletin board in Charlotte, February

CHAPTER FOUR

"Glad everyone could make it."

Donald Stabler surveyed the conference room. Around the walnut table sat six men and one woman at various stages of attention. They all had legal pads and pens lined up on the table in front of them. Their expressions were that of soliders hunkered down in their trenches waiting for the crossfire to begin. Mugs of coffee steamed, producing a biting aroma that hung over the oval conference table like a morning mist.

Donald loved these meetings. He never tired of the sound of his own voice. And he enjoyed the look on his employees' faces as they fought panic in the moments between the time a question left his mouth and the time it took for them to think of a suitable answer. Sort of reminded Donald of deer caught in the headlights.

That was okay. Business was a war and he, Donald Stabler, would always be the winner. He might lose a skirmish or two, but like that great military genius Douglas MacArthur, he always returned. And when he did, he conquered.

Walter sat to his left, fiddling with some sort of electronic organizer, totally absorbed in the numbers flashing across the screen. His only child and yet, the way Walter acted sometimes made Donald wonder if the genetic code had somehow been altered. The boy just didn't have what it took some days. He lacked Donald's killer instinct. It had to be Martha's family, they had some simpletons mixed in there somewhere. Sooner or later those defective genes broke through.

The sleek conference room had been decorated by Martha, Donald's ex-wife. 'Ex-wife' was a problem since Martha didn't seem to understand the concept of ex-wife. She called him constantly to complain about one thing or another. The roofers that he sent didn't fix the roof right, the monthly divorce settlement payment was late, Walter didn't visit often enough. Donald felt he was very patient with her, explaining again and again what the concept of divorce meant and reminding her that Walter was an adult now. Then he would mention to Walter that his mother was calling again. This scenario played itself out on a regular basis.

Donald breathed a sigh of relief when Martha had decided to take a six-month cruise with her sister. Six months of peace and quiet. He would never admit to anyone, least of all himself, that he missed having someone at the house—not Martha, but someone. However, there was an upside to having no one else at home. All his energy could be focused on the business, on the battlefield.

He tapped his fingers impatiently on the table as he turned to discuss the latest P and Ls with Walter.

• • • • • • • • •

Larry Adams held a printout from the previous quarter. He had been staring at the same page for the last ten minutes, sipping coffee and praying this meeting would be short. If 'The Donald,' as his staff referred to him when he was not present, thought that he was going to have Adams' people off chasing after his crazy notions, he could forget it. They barely had time to breathe, what with trying to get two new companies on board, systems switched over, and issues still to be worked out from the Kinton acquisition. Denise Burton, who headed the Information Technology group, complained daily that she could not get the new distribution and manufacturing guys to really listen to her. They kept screwing up the system and doing things that cost the company extra money – money Adams was going to get eaten alive for.

Now, 'The Donald' wanted them to help logistics. Right. Adams was going to focus his resources on logistics. Let logistics take care of themselves.

• • • • • • • • •

On the left side of the conference table, John O'Connor listened as Denise Burton talked about an MRP II system that she hoped to get Donald Stabler's approval for in the next few weeks. It would be one more thing that personnel in the plants would have to be trained to do, but Denise chattered on, pointing out the best features of the system, oblivious to John's less-than-ecstatic response. This electronic voodoo stuff was great, John thought, but you had to get everybody singing from the same page or you were wasting your time. He had a friend whose company spent thousands developing information technology, but it sat idle now because no one else had the computer capability to interface with their "Star Wars" execution.

John hoped he could get a few minutes with Rich Morrison. Rich's people were developing some type of team-based operation and Walter kept throwing it up in John's face. Usually if Walter liked something, John counted it as useless. Stabler had already been through that team thing a couple of times and John's people had tried them. Like all that stuff, teams eventually faded into the background and manufacturing went back to business as usual. John figured he'd better at least see what he could do to make it look like his group was doing something. Walter was buzzing around these days like a bumblebee on steroids.

The little voice outside his head stopped. Denise Burton was looking at him. He realized that she had paused to give him a chance to make comment.

"That sounds very interesting. Will your people provide training?"

● ● ● ● ● ● ● ● ●

Denise Burton noticed the glaze come over John's eyes the minute she started talking about the new MRP II system. Why did these management-types resist new technology so much? If she could just package the stuff like an electronic game and name it something like 'Master of Disaster III,' they'd fight for the chance to learn how it worked. John was not the worst by far; he seemed very distracted today. Given the way 'The Donald' was tapping his fingers on the table, she could understand why.

● ● ● ● ● ● ● ● ●

Rich Morrison stared at the printing on the side of his pen. Next to him, Marcus Warren and Raymond Rodriquez sat side-by-side, each trying to impress the other with their knowledge of specialty coffees. Marcus described a double latte that he had had in Seattle recently in terms that were close to orgasmic. Raymond topped him with a double mocha espresso. It was yuppie war at its bloodiest. Rich wouldn't have been surprised if they challenged each other to a duel with their espresso machines.

Rich looked up and realized that of the eight people gathered around the table, only Donald Stabler looked at ease. Everyone else tried to disguise their sense of dread by conversing with those around them or reading reports pulled from their briefcases.

Rich thought of Melissa. He had been so shocked on Tuesday night by her proposal of a new baby that they had very little discussion on the issue. In fact, when she had seen the look on Rich's face, Melissa had laughed and said, "Just think about it and get back to me." But it wasn't her 'only kidding' laugh. She was serious, or thought she was, about having another baby.

• • • • • • • • •

Donald Stabler's voice brought the quiet hum of conversation to a halt.

"What I'm proposing is simple, really. Each division is going to be called on to support the redesign of distribution. It's time we all realized this is a key issue to our success. And I want you to understand how I feel about it." Donald slapped the table with the heel of his hand to emphasize his words. "It's vital. And Rich's plate is full. I know that because I filled it." Donald chuckled at his own joke.

"He needs all the support we can give him to bring these distribution issues in line. We've got to cut inventory, and at the same time we've got to give customers what they want, when they want it. Logistics must become a core competency at Stabler."

Raymond Rodriquez spoke up. "With all due respect to sales and marketing and, of course, the customer, planning is in such a state, I don't know what we can do to support Rich. Every few months, Nandy and her bunch of designers try to wipe out our entire line and start from scratch."

Nandy Gamble was head of the Fashion Design Team that worked for Marcus Warren in sales and marketing. Raymond's sarcastic tone indicated his disdain for Ms. Gamble and her crew, as well as the fact that he was still smarting from the coffee war.

He continued, "My budget is shot to hell and the DC guys are screaming because they have warehouses full of things that are not only not selling, they are being returned faster than tacky ties after Father's Day. So the DC guys have got to figure out how to stack all the returns. Then everyone comes after me because none of our customers have what they want."

Larry Adams spoke up. "I'm telling you, we've got to invest in the technology. With everyone we're bringing on board, our current systems can hardly keep up with payroll, let alone our information needs. My people have been looking at a centralized system for months. We just need the green light."

"What kind of centralized system?" Rich asked.

"Total operations. One that links us throughout the country and with our overseas ops. We transmit our manufacturing schedule and they can send us advance shipping notices. Then Rich's people can be ready to roll when the goods arrive. With one of these enterprise-wide systems, information is out there for everyone. With total operations, manufacturing, warehousing, and shipments being tracked, we can network the warehousing and manufacturing operations into the main system." Larry snapped his fingers. "Ba de bing, ba de bang, the sales people can call up inventory numbers and Rich's people can call up sales."

"Shouldn't we be concerned about proprietary or confidential information?" Walter asked.

"Oh, come on, Walter, you're talking to finance here. Employees won't have access to that kind of information. I look at it this way, we're sure not going to get any better keeping people in the dark."

Walter looked skeptical. "Not that it wouldn't hurt them to know some of our numbers. I mean let's do a quick review of operations. Do you know that power bills are up significantly at all our sites? I thought we were installing those gizmos that regulated the building temperature and lights. Larry, I seem to remember that we were promised an ROI of thirty-six percent, after tax, on those things."

"To my knowledge, we never installed them. The facilities people put in all the paperwork, but the system wasn't approved."

"I approved it." Walter cut his eyes at Larry, daring him to disagree.

"I'll have to check with Carol in purchasing, but as of last Friday, the facilities people were still screaming because they hadn't gotten the go-ahead. Didn't Dan Goldman call you?"

Walter seemed to light up temporarily. "So that's why Dan was calling me. I wondered about that." He frowned again. "I could have sworn I approved that purchase."

"I haven't seen any signatures," Larry said.

Rich sighed to himself. Any minute now they were going to start with, "Yes, I did. No, you didn't."

"What the hell are you doing in the loop anyway, Walter?" Donald turned and confronted his son.

"Donald, you know we agreed that major expenditures like that needed upper-level approval."

Rich leaned back in his chair as the great finance debate roared on. How was he going to redesign the complete logistics process, hell, maybe even the entire company with this kind of yanging over energy management for plant maintenance. Blah, Blah, yada, yada.

"Rich." The sound of his name pulled him back into the discussion.

"—controlling expense is a major issue. For instance, office supplies are eating us up."

Rich realized that Walter was on his favorite soapbox. He wasn't going to be required to say anything. It was one of the speeches Walter gave on a regular basis. In fact, Rich had heard it so often, that if Walter were to be beamed up by aliens in mid-speech, Rich could finish it for him. For Walter, office supplies were the root of all evil. Everything from the fall of ancient Rome to the Hindenberg disaster could be traced to a line item—office supplies. Yet they didn't even make up a percentage point of the logistics budget. Rich wished he had a nickel for every time he and Walter talked about this. It would probably cover his office supply budget twice over. What would it take to get Walter off his soapbox?

Donald. He let Walter go on for about three more sentences before he interrupted.

"Let's step back and try to look at the big picture here. Individual budget issues, you and Larry review on a case-by-case basis."

"Well, sure. I was just pointing out a problem area that I think is a symptom of something much bigger."

Office supplies, the cancer of the corporate world. Silently invading and destroying your budget. Rich wanted to scream.

Donald ignored Walter's last statement. "What about manufacturing, John? Walter tells me you're running behind with your ISO 9000 certification schedule."

"Walter's right. We are running behind. However, a lot of it has to do with what Raymond mentioned earlier. Our resources are tapped out on other things. The number of new product designs being generated are impossible for us to keep up with. We have a couple of suppliers that are cheaper but don't deliver the goods on time. It seems to me that whatever it is we're saving on that end, we're more than spending trying to make up for their slack delivery."

"Aren't we imposing penalties on these people?" Donald asked.

"Yes. But quite frankly, that doesn't do me any good when I've got Marcus and Rich breathing down my neck," John said.

"I'm only breathing down his neck because I've got our clients dancing a jig on my head, threatening to pull contracts and imposing penalties which come out of my budget because their order didn't ship on time or it was short. You can't ship imaginary products. I'm not trying to place blame, but the penalties are going to come back against the DCs," Rich said.

"Then, like I pointed out before, they all come after me because I didn't plan well enough," Raymond added. "And how can I plan when we're putting a gazillion new items out on the market every day? Items with no history. I don't know if I should be buying a truckload of red lace or three truckloads of black satin or if all the women in the United States are going to go PC on us and demand green cotton."

"Green underwear. I've never heard of green underwear," Walter smirked.

"Walter, green cotton is not green. It's cotton grown without chemicals," Raymond said.

Rich closed his eyes. The distribution issue was not going to be fixed by itself. It simply represented one part of the supply chain. That in itself was a problem. If each area represented a link, then each area thought of itself as an entity on its own which produced the attitude 'as long as I'm looking out for my link, to hell with yours.' No wonder Donald put him in charge of revamping the system. He was the guy who would get clobbered by the penalties if things didn't straighten up. Somehow Rich had to get the others to see the process as one smooth flow from start to finish. So who would volunteer to have the penalties added to their budget? Sure, they'd be pushing and shoving to sign up for that, all right.

Ignoring Donald's tapping fingers, Walter continued to plod through operational minutia as if somehow that would produce a revelation from on high. Rich doodled on his legal pad and thought of what it would take to get this project moving. It seemed as if he needed to attack it from several directions. For instance, one of the new operations Donald Stabler had acquired used a third-party firm for all its distribution needs. Rich's contact at the third-party assured him that it reduced his cost and gave his operation greater logistics expertise and improved customer service. Rich wasn't so sure how a third-party system would work at the other distribution centers. He knew that many of his present employees would resist a new player in the distribution cycle. And then there was control. He couldn't control what happened now, so how would he control a third-party?

When the meeting was over, Rich caught up with Marcus Warren in the hall. "Marcus, why didn't you let me know what was going on with the Whitehead account? The first I hear of the trouble, they're almost ready to yank the account."

"Rich, it's like Donald said in there. Everything needs to be revamped. But I've been on the phone with Walter almost weekly about Whitehead. He said he'd talk to you."

"Do me a favor, Marcus, from now on just talk to me. Go ahead and skip the middleman."

Rich went back to the conference room, but he didn't have a chance to talk to Walter alone. Instead, he and Donald and Walter talked about the Whitehead account. Walter denied having conversations with Marcus. When Rich pressed him, he admitted, "Okay, maybe once or twice."

Rich asked Donald about the specifics of his conversation with Howie Whitehead. He learned that what Whitehead wanted was a primary vendor who could give them the 'perfect order.' One hundred percent fill rate on the first shipment, on-time delivery, perfect pricing including promotions and proper carton labels for each store.

"We're in the perfect striking position for this, Rich. And we're getting ready to lose it. Think of all the product lines we're carrying now."

Donald didn't have to tell him about new product lines. The problem wasn't quantity, the problem was giving customers what they wanted.

"Donald, I can't fill what I don't have. We've got to get something worked out with manufacturing. Rodriquez is right. We're sitting on warehouses full of duds while the customers are screaming for things we don't have. Plus we're trying to incorporate two new DCs into the company along with all their product lines. And you heard John O'Connor, manufacturing has a couple of vendors that are killing them," Rich said.

"Rich, that's what I want you to fix. I'll expect a plan no later than a week from today outlining how to up this seventy-two percent order-fulfillment rate. If I like what I see, then you'll get the resources. After that, Walter will keep me apprised of how this reorganization effort is going. If people are throwing up roadblocks, Walter is there to help and to let me know if I need to step in, but you're really out there on your own," Donald said.

Walter isn't just a roadblock, Rich thought, he is a blown-up bridge. But how to tell his father—that's the real challenge.

"I'll want reports, but what I really want is results. I'm going to give you enough rope to hang yourself with. How about it?" Donald grinned.

"That's great, Donald. But we'll need enough time to get the teaming effort functioning. I need to take one facility and work with the DC and manufacturing to redesign operations. Then we can change our entire network."

"Time is a limited commodity. We're being outgunned. We've got to flank them now."

Rich always got the feeling that he was in the command tent just back from enemy lines when he talked with Donald. Often when he left these meetings, he felt shell-shocked. Rich's exasperation showed in his voice.

"We can't move forward with some half-assed plans. Yes, we need to move. Yes, we need to make sure we're looking to the future, but we can't spend our time fortifying outdated systems. The French were routed at the Maginot Line because they thought they were invincible. They'd fortified a system all right, but they didn't have the vision to see the wave of the future, the air war."

"My point exactly. Which is why I'm expecting you to be our distribution visionary. The Napoleon of Stabler Distribution. I like you, Rich, but when Howie Whitehead starts looking to give the lion's share of his shelf space to other lingerie manufacturers and distributors, we've got problems. Nine months—I'll give you nine months to show significant improvement above and beyond what these other guys are doing. Otherwise, I'm going to have all the DC managers report directly to Walter. He'll call the shots."

In three sentences, Donald had gone from calling him Napoleon (pre-Waterloo, Rich assumed), to telling him he had nine months before Walter took over the heart of the logistics operations.

But not if Rich could improve the operation.

GOOSE CHASE

"I hate change. It makes me have to turn off my brain's automatic pilot and actually start thinking about how to do my job."

— Lucretia Haddock to Janet Gordon at the First Baptist Church's Valentine's Day potluck dinner, February

CHAPTER FIVE

"You're listening to the BUZZ—104.2 on your FM dial. Traffic is a mess on the east side and an accident on the 770 expressway has everything tied up in both directions. Avoid it if you can. Aren't you glad it's Friday?"

Rich eased the Suburban into a line of merging traffic on the parkway. It seemed like only a few minutes since he'd stepped off the late flight from Boston. Arriving home past midnight, the laws of physics suspended themselves. One minute he pulled the covers over his head, and the next the radio alarm sounded in his ear, the chirpy announcer almost too much to bear.

The note Melissa had left him on the kitchen table was stuck to the Suburban's dashboard in front of him.

"Carrot cake is in the fridge. Don't forget Andrew has a scrimmage Friday night. Try to make it if you can. I got the offer from Sewell & Prather today. Made a copy for you to look over. Maybe we can talk about it as we pass each other in the hallway. I love you."

Rich had the proposal in his briefcase, not certain when he would have a chance to look at it. Last night, he had polished off a big hunk of carrot cake, which was his favorite, before climbing the stairs and getting ready for bed. He made as little noise as possible. Even so, Melissa had stirred when he got in the bed. When he asked her what she thought of the proposal, her answer was muffled in the pillow. He kissed her lightly on her cheek and she acknowledged the gesture by lifting her hand up off the pillow for a brief moment and muttering something like "twek bstslelc you" into the pillow. As the note said, maybe they would have a chance to talk about the offer in the hallway.

The driver of the car in front of the Suburban slammed on his brakes, waking Rich out of his auto-pilot state.

"This is Jack Thompson, your man with the business answers. Tonight, during drive time on the BUZZ, tune in for my program featuring renowned quality expert, Mike Mayes. Mike has the answers to your quality problems. He and his team at QualityWorks have implemented quality solutions in several hundred companies. He'll join me taking your calls and answering the hard questions. For a 'quality' difference in your work tomorrow, join me at six for 'The Jack Thompson Show' today."

A feminine voice followed, "This is Micki. Spice up your life and join me for 'Micki's Place' where we'll hear from women and men who say, 'I Was a Plastic Surgery Failure.'"

Rich swung into the parking lot. He had Barbara arrange for his Leadership Team to get together first thing this morning. If they were going to make a revolution happen, it would take a commitment from everyone. The Leadership Team included Valerie Wagner from personnel, George Nader from quality, Rachel Alvarado from customer service, Irving Steed from traffic and Bob Ketchum.

Enough brain power existed in the group to lead a revolution. They just needed to be pointed in the right direction. Rich needed for them to understand the urgency they worked under, but he also knew he walked a fine line between motivating them and scaring them so badly that they would start updating their resumes.

No one moved as Rich described his meeting at Stabler headquarters. He ended by saying, "We can do it, but we must pull together if we are going to transform the process."

"To what?" Bob said.

"Well, that's our challenge to figure out 'to what.' We know what's wrong. If a customer goes into a store, they have absolutely got to find what they want. The Stabler brand in the right color and the right size. If not, they walk or they go look at Jockey or Calvin Klein to see who has the comparable product. We lose a sale, and the store starts looking at which vendors have the item on the shelf when the customer wants it."

"But the stores are so damn picky. On hangers, off hangers, stickers, no stickers," Bob complained, waving his hands in frustration.

"You've got to look at it this way, Bob. They're one step closer to the customer. It's through the screamers that we get the information that drives our whole process.

"The sale of ten pairs of women's gray cotton boxers should tell us to ship ten more pairs, and that in turn should tell manufacturing to make ten more pairs, and that in turn should be transmitted to our supplier of gray cotton cloth which leads him to produce more."

"That's all well and good, but we're not meeting our ship schedules now. How can we possibly expect to work backward and do it?" Rachel Alvarado looked puzzled.

"Exactly, Rachel, we can't do it the way we are and stay competitive. We have no choice with over four hundred Stabler SKUs in a store. Demand flow logistics is the only answer."

"Demand flow logistics?"

"We've got to pull our product through a pipeline in a smooth, quick way. If you turn on the faucet in your kitchen, you expect clear, clean water. That's just the way our product should flow. When the customer turns on the tap in a Whitehead's department store, they should be able to get the Stabler product they expect."

"We can't ship what we haven't got. And manufacturing isn't interested in hearing our problems." Bob leaned back and crossed his arms over his chest.

"Well they are now because Donald Stabler told them they're interested."

Irving Steed threw his hands into the air. "This is not one of my problems. I've been trying to get the IT people to help me with the new software we need for customs. If they've got time to do this, they've got time to get on with what I need. I mean, if you guys are going to help me solve the issues we're facing with the 'MOD Act,' then I'll start working on coming up with great ideas for this pipeline thing."

George Nader shook his head. "The MOD Squad is the least of our troubles. I'd say we've got big-time quality issues. And I can't get the people on the Quality Team to do squat. Who is going to do something about that?"

Problems with the Quality Team didn't surprise Rich, given George's attitude.

Valerie Wagner laughed. "George and Irving, are you working with us or against us? George, you hadn't mentioned problems with the Quality Team. I'll be glad to see if I can help unstick the process. If we all don't get in this together, it can't happen."

"It's true. No silo management. We've got to work together." Rich agreed. "Irving, since you're having trouble with the IT area, why don't you work with me to evaluate the system they want to put in place?"

"Okay, but I'm telling you I've got to get some support from those people." Irving said.

"I've given this a lot of thought. We need to benchmark what others are doing. I think that Bob and Rachel should check out at least two other operations. We can take that information and use it as a jumping-off point for developing our new process. Then I'm going to propose a cross-functional team to handle the Whitehead account. A group dedicated to making sure the Whitehead stores get what they want and more."

"That makes sense, but are we going to be able to do that with every account we have?" Rachel asked.

"Whitehead's red hot right now, and we've got to start somewhere. The Rollins account needs attention too, but I think I can buy us a little more time with them." Rich made himself a note to talk with Marcus Warren about the Rollins account.

"Meanwhile, as I said, the information technology people have the system they are recommending that can generate the kind of real-time information we need to have to do demand flow."

"Who's going to be on the Whitehead Team?"

"I've got to run it by Walter and Donald first. First shot, I think someone from customer service, sales, marketing, manufacturing, planning, distribution, and finance. That covers every area of the company that the Whitehead stores deal with.

"The Whitehead account isn't the only issue, it's a symptom of bigger ones. That's why I'm concerned that our teams here in-house be given enough time to demonstrate their real success. Again, it's going to require everyone in this room letting go of territory. And Valerie, you'll need to check with every team, the leaders and the liaisons to see where they stand in fulfilling their charters."

Irving tapped his pencil on the table. "Excuse me, Rich, but I want to go back to the benchmarking issue. I just can't see the value in that. You don't remember, but a year or so before Stabler bought Kinton, we tried to do that with manufacturing. It was a mess."

"How so?"

"Well, one of the guys who used to work for me transferred over to manufacturing. He said they were so busy trying to copy what some jeans manufacturer had been doing two years earlier, it almost put us out of business. Anyway, by the time you get a system installed, it's two years since the other guy was doing it that way. Sort of like every company in the United States thinking they had to copy the way the Japanese put on their pants."

"Good point, Irving. However, what I'd like for us to do is use the information we get from benchmarking to look at what we are doing to help us see our own system in a new way, not to copy someone else's."

Irving ignored Rich. "What I want to know is what does jeans production have to do with us? The numbers don't do us any good."

"Again, Irving, another good point. We're not benchmarking for numbers, we're benchmarking for process. "

"If we don't do the numbers, how will we know if we succeeded?"

"We need our own measures. But measuring our numbers against someone else's is not the answer. We should be measuring ourselves against the customer's expectations."

Irving looked unhappy.

Rich continued, "If we decided to benchmark in-house—let's say we looked at second shift. If we use easy round numbers and say we've got a picker on second shift who is sending out $80,000 in product a night. So she is shipping $10,000 per man hour. We make that our goal. So we go to first shift and we tell the picker that our target is $10,000 per man hour. He laughs. Why? Because he is picking replenishment orders for smaller customers—he does well to ship $1,000 per man hour, let alone $10,000. So we hang around until our 'super-picker' on second shift comes in. Come to find out what second shift is doing is filling orders for our mass market items with major retailers. They're picking almost by the pallet, while first shift is picking pretty much by the piece. The order profiles are completely different. So even in our own operation, if we use the wrong numbers as a benchmarking method, we're screwing up the process."

Irving did not look convinced. "If we're not getting their numbers and we're not getting their systems, aren't we wasting our time?"

"No, because what we're looking for is that 'aha.' That spark that helps us see what we're doing in a whole new light. That's what I hope Rachel and George will do. And by sharing what they have seen with the rest of us, who knows?" Rich said.

"I'm all for that, but how can we make demand flow work for us when we don't even know all our products right now?" George tried to look a little less defensive in the light of Valerie's earlier point.

"We're going to start small. Our basic line first, then we can expand to our other products. Give this your priority. I'll write the team charter and then we can discuss our ideas for team members before I get input on that from Walter and Donald. Let's meet again same time on Tuesday."

Bob Ketchum stayed behind as the others left.

"So give it to me straight. Is Walter calling the shots?"

"No, but we're up against it. It's change or die."

GOOSE CHASE

"A change is as good as a rest."

— Louise Cross to her granddaughter,
Hilary, while Hilary was giving
Louise a perm, Louise's kitchen,
February

CHAPTER SIX

Friday evening, Rich headed in the direction of the school for Andrew's game. At the stoplight by the DC, he stopped drumming his fingers on the steering wheel long enough to switch on the radio.

"Today on the show my guest is Mike Mayes, general manager of QualityWorks. Mike has over thirty years of various quality and business systems background. For the past six years at QualityWorks, he has aided companies in improving their business positions through the implementation of structured quality systems. Now that's a mouthful. Mike, what does it all really mean?"

"Actually, Jack, it's very simple. All businesses can benefit from having, at some level, a set of quality or management practices that give them some assurance that the future can be predicted."

"If you can predict the future, I'm out of radio and into quality. You must be kidding."

Mike laughed. "No, I'm not. But don't quit your day job yet. All I am saying is that many companies, and for that matter many families, have lost the edge of discipline to have actions repeated in a manner that recurs from day to day. It's like Mark Twain once said, 'Without banks, a river is just a puddle.'

"Let me give you an example. One company I worked with, a few months back, had a problem mixing up orders from their customers. They kept shipping the right stuff on the right day to the wrong address. I mean, on a regular basis, not a week went by without a missed shipment or three."

"I bet they had some unhappy customers."

"You're right about that. Anyway, they asked us to look at their systems and we found some very simple items they could improve right off the bat to stop the errors. A very easy one was to redesign their sales order format. Their sales force couldn't note on the old form if there was a difference in billing, shipping and correspondence addresses. We reworked the forms and the database in their computer system to clarify the different addresses and went to zero missed shipments almost overnight."

"So with a simple form and computer redesign you provided for your client's future. In other words, that they would have predictable shipments. Is that right?"

"Yes. But that was only the tip of the iceberg. The leaders of the business looked around and asked themselves, and us, if this type of error is happening in our order entry, what other problems do we have?"

"And what did you say?"

"We asked if they would commission a GAP analysis of their present operation to a standard to allow a comparison to known good practices."

"And did they?"

"Absolutely. The momentum of change was propelling them now. So we did a three-day study of their quality management systems using ISO 9002 as a standard."

"I thought the ISO standards were only for manufacturing companies."

"No, the ISO 9000 standards can be applied to any business that produces a product or a service. They represent a good basic set of practices for a company to use to standardize or stabilize a set of working conditions."

"And did they live happily ever after? How did it end?"

"The end is always the next beginning. It never ends. They did implement a quality management system based upon ISO 9002. We received recognition for it by an independent auditor. Our client realizes that they have started a journey for quality improvement that has no finish line."

"Hang on folks, we'll be right back to take your questions for Mike after this message from Compusystems."

When the show returned from the commercial, the first caller wanted to know about the differences between the Baldrige award and ISO 9000.

"It's like the difference between the Olympics and a driver's license," Mike replied.

"I see the connection between the Olympics and quality, but the driver in front of me on the beltway this morning definitely didn't know what the word 'quality' meant in relation to the driving experience. Explain," Jack said.

"At the driver's license level, almost anyone can study the books and practice driving to the point where they can pass a state test. That's certainly how you felt about the other driver this morning. That is sort of like getting a basic ISO 9003 registration certificate. The ISO 9003 only covers a minimal system of inspections and management systems. Almost any company with a bit of learning and discipline can be ISO 9003 certified or registered."

"That's interesting. My impression has been that ISO is very hard for some companies to achieve."

"Well, as companies need more of their business practices covered by a registration standard, we move up to ISO 9002 and 9001. These are more involved. With 9002, it covers a company's ability to demonstrate a series of controls over order taking, making the product or doing the service, and then shipping the materials to the right place at the right time. It also encompasses the actions a company takes in purchasing raw materials, corrective actions and audits. If we go back to our driver's license example, it is like getting a motor-cycle endorsement added to your basic license. Many states have an added test to prove your ability to drive a bike.

"Then we go on to commercial driver's licenses. More learning, more testing. That's ISO 9001. The scope of ISO 9001 takes into account the control companies have over their new products or services design processes. To obtain an ISO 9001 registration, you must get the right products to the marketplace with tests all completed. Then the customer or consumer can buy the product with confidence."

"Okay. But where do the Olympics and the Baldrige come in?"

"Well, if there was an Olympic driving event it would go like this. You train for years, you qualify in stages and then you get one shot every fourth year. The Baldrige is like that. The Baldrige criteria ask for data that prove your company has done their training and prequalification by looking at three to five years of evidence that you provide to them."

"No easy task."

"That's right, Jack. But remember, one of their criteria's values is in serving as a benchmark. The criteria they provide can give you some good guidance on how to improve your company's operation. It's been distilled from years of research as to what it takes to be a successful American company."

"So how the company operates is the key?"

"One of the keys. A good set of business practices can go a long way, but a company has to have a good product or service that the marketplace needs. A well-managed buggy-whip company will not last long in today's market. As you can imagine, no demand."

The next caller referred to an earlier program on supplier management programs. "I wondered if Mike had any thoughts on that issue?"

"No company can get better than the weakest supplier in the flow to your facility. The companies that are fully integrated with their suppliers, being partners in the flow of products and services, to them will be the strongest in the future. Both companies benefit when they have a supplier partnership process with shared risks and rewards.

"What do you mean by shared rewards?"

"It makes sense that when a supplier clearly knows your needs and consistently exceeds them, they should be recognized with a stronger business relationship. This relationship could mean a bigger share of the purchases you make or even being a sole source of selected services or products for you, some reward for helping your business grow. The time you save by only dealing with selected suppliers can be spent improving other aspects of your operation which is another bonus to your firm."

"But with suppliers, won't an ISO certification by a company guarantee good products?" The caller asked.

"No. Because ISO certification in the various 9000 series standards will only serve to give a leg up on consistency in how various management practices are performed. The ISO 9000 series doesn't certify the products."

The next caller had to ask his question three times because his cellular phone transmission kept breaking up his words. Finally, the two men deciphered his question.

"Let's hope your cellular company is listening to our quality show," Jack joked and repeated the caller's question, 'So how is a quality system different from a business system?'"

"Great question," Mike replied. "It isn't. A quality system and a business system should be one and the same. Over the years, we've lost a lot of logic in our business schools and so quality systems and business systems have become separated. A company that fully integrates quality and business factors is a better-managed company."

"So how did this separation occur?" Jack asked.

"It evolved. As quality grew more complex, it became a function of trying to catch the guys in the back of the shop trying to ship defective goods. Management built gun ships out of the quality departments which separated them even further.

"Then management challenged production to make as much stuff as possible, and kick it up two or three notches like that famous 'I Love Lucy' scene where Ethel and Lucy are supposed to be packing candy. As production increases, they end up with candy in their aprons and in their mouths. Before it's all over, candy is everywhere. So back at our company, production is stepped up and then the quality department is deputized to stop any bad stuff from leaving.

"There is a way to avoid this mentality. In a company where production and quality are the primary responsibility of the production department, where warrantees are charged back to production and not some marketing or quality account, you are more likely to see a cohesive system in place. Or as I say—a team that is all on the same journey to greatness, using the same map."

Rich picked up his cell phone and dialed in the show's number. In a few seconds, his voice was on the air.

"I'm in a company where order fulfillment is an issue. It's a multi-site situation and I'm having trouble getting straight answers to what is going on and why. We have no consistent approach."

"This multi-site situation—how did it come about? Mergers, rapid growth, acquisitions?"

"Mostly acquisitions."

"Well, sometimes problems come about because of rapid growth or acquisitions. This often happens as geography puts distances between the plants or places of business. A company's culture is a very difficult thing to transfer."

"It sure is. We were a great little place with a good consistent process, then we started buying up competitors and others whose business aligned with ours," Rich said.

"It sounds like you need a model for regaining some of the consistency of practices that were traditions in the original business." Mike said.

"How do we get to that model?"

"You need to seek out the best practices and model them between locations. That will take some education as well as hard work."

"I think we're working hard now, we're just not working smart. Education couldn't hurt us. Any suggestions?" Rich asked.

"At the end of the show, I'll give you an address to write to for more information. In your case, I'll send you a monograph on the use of ISO in a warehousing business," Mike said.

Jack added, "It sounds like you're mobile, Rich. If you miss that address, our switchboard here at the station will have it on file. Now Mike, would you give us a short summary of all we've covered? We've covered everything but what I call quality, which is, will my car last forever and will my wife's cooking get any better?"

"The definition of quality is one of the biggest problems we face. In this country, we don't seem to have a handle on the concept of quality. What is it? 'Quality,' as a word, has been misused and abused by all of us. It is like the word 'beautiful.' It defies definition because its meaning to all of us is so personal. If, for instance, we think of your car, that's product quality. Will it perform in a reliable manner? If we're speaking of your wife's cooking, do you have a set of clearly defined expectations? And does she have her own expectations for how well you keep the garage cleaned out?

"We need to shift away from using the word 'quality,' and instead use the core factors we are seeking. A system for doing the right things in business is a business system, not a quality system. Your expectation that your car will get you home is automotive reliability. The problems with your bank getting your checks deposited in the right account is account management and the accounting practices of your bank. None of these are quality, but if our expectations aren't met, we think of them all as bad quality.

"Quality as a concept is a journey. As I said earlier, it never ends. We strive tomorrow to do a better quality job than we did today. Keep getting better and better. The world will beat a path to your door when you build a better mousetrap."

"Thanks, Mike. That wraps it up for tonight. Join me on Monday when my guest will be Randall Heisling, vice president of LogisticsWorks, one of the largest third-party logistics providers in the world."

Rich turned off the radio as the strains of Micki's theme song began. At the high school, the sounds of the cheerleaders echoed from the gym down the hallway's tiled floor. Andrew played on the varsity squad for Wilder High School. As a sophomore, he wasn't seeing a lot of playing time but seemed to improve with every game, gaining experience and confidence as he went along.

Rich arrived midway through the first half as the visiting team called a time-out. Cheerleaders ran onto the floor in a swirl of red and blue pompoms and blue uniforms, smiles pasted across their faces. Rich wondered if they ever wanted to say, "Who cares?" and walk away.

Melissa waved to him from the stands. She wore jeans and a Wilder High School sweatshirt, looking more like a soccer mom than an advertising executive. The man next to her turned and waved, motioning Rich on up the bleachers. What the hell was J. Thomas Sewell doing here now?

"As Arnold H. Glasou said, 'The trouble with the future is that it usually arrives before we are ready for it.' In our case—that may be an understatement."

— Rich Morrison to the Leadership Team at Stabler, February

CHAPTER SEVEN

Rich quickly scanned the area around Sewell for Kelly, but she was not there. Making his way up the bleachers, Rich sat down and kissed Melissa before he leaned around to acknowledge Sewell's presence.

"Hi stranger, how are you?" Melissa smiled.

"Doing great. Where's Kelly?"

Melissa must have read his thoughts, she patted his hand. "Sitting down the way with some of her friends. She's going with Jake for pizza after the game. They're going to Pizza Warehouse."

Jake Oliver was a senior on the school's basketball team. Rich teased Kelly about him all the time when they first started dating, calling him 'Jake the Rake.' Jake seemed to be at their house more than he was at his own, and Rich had grown accustomed to having him around. Recalling Kelly's dreamy description of Thomas the other night, Jake looked better all the time.

"Thomas, this is a surprise. Are you scouting for college teams on the side now or looking for a date?" Rich smiled.

Thomas threw back his head and laughed so hard he missed seeing the elbow Melissa poked into Rich's ribcage.

"Neither. When I was over at the house the other day, we were talking about Andrew and basketball. You know I remember him when he was coming along, a little tike actually. Hard to imagine him over six feet now. So I thought I'd come out and see a little of the game. On a more selfish level, keep that bug in Melissa's ear about our offer."

"Honestly, Thomas, I just got the proposal late yesterday."

The buzzer sounded and both teams walked back out on the floor, saving Rich from a response. The rest of the half went quickly with Andrew subbing a number of minutes. When the buzzer sounded for half-time, Thomas stood.

"Good to see you again. I've got a late date for the Hornet's game—Annalise Latham. You might remember her. She was Miss North Carolina a few years ago. She is on a modeling assignment and couldn't make the game until the second half. I'm on my way to get her now. That Andrew is quite a player. I'll put in a good word with George Shinn if you'd like."

Rich resisted the urge to ask if Annalise was Tiny Miss North Carolina.

"Right, you do that. But only if the Hornets win tonight."

Thomas smiled and nodded. "Look forward to hearing from you soon, Melissa." He leaned over and gave Melissa a 'love you, mean it' hug, the equivalent of the air kiss.

As soon as Thomas was down the bleachers, Rich said, "So is he incapable of using a telephone, a fax machine, or any other form of communication except face-to-face?"

Melissa waved her hand as if she were shooing away a gnat. "The guys are just nervous, that's all. I haven't been all over this proposal like they thought I would be."

"Well, I'm starting to wonder if he's more interested in your business or in you. You haven't told him about this baby thing, have you? Maybe that's why he is hanging around."

Melissa turned her back and didn't speak to him the rest of the game, carrying on cheerful conversations with several couples around them. Rich watched the game. Even with the heat of the crowd in the gym, he could feel the cold radiating his way from Melissa's shoulder.

Andrew got beat by a power forward on the other team two times in a row, giving the guy easy lay-ups. The coach pulled Andrew. He sat, his head hung down, at the end of the bench. Wilder barely won the game.

When the final buzzer sounded, Kelly appeared from somewhere in the jubilant crowd.

"Jake and I will give Andrew a ride if you guys want to go ahead home."

"That's great, honey. How about you drive your Mom's car home for me so she and I can ride together?"

Melissa buttoned her jacket without looking up.

"No. There's no need for Kelly to worry about that. I feel like driving, and I need to stop by the market anyway. There's some chicken scallopini and a salad in the refrigerator. I've already eaten, so don't wait for me."

Kelly flipped her hand. "Whatever. We'll still give him a ride."

At the house, Rich changed out of his suit into a sweatshirt and jeans, found his dinner and thought about his day. The Leadership Team had been fairly receptive. That was a good first step. Rich knew there were going to be some bumps along the way. No doubt about that. So the question was, could the group come together in spite of those bumps? Rich wondered. At some point over the weekend, he had to get the proposed membership and the charter for the Whitehead Team down on paper for Donald and Walter. Next week he would need to spend some time working with Larry Adams and Denise Burton to see what could be done about that software system, and work with Valerie in Charlotte to smooth the way for the teams at the DC. Plus he had to fight any fires that came with the territory.

He knew he needed to make the time on Saturday to shoot basketball with Andrew as he had promised on Tuesday. Rich swallowed a bite of chicken—Tuesday seemed years ago.

Also on Saturday evening, he and Melissa were supposed to go to dinner with a couple whom they knew from their college days. Mark and Patty were driving through Charlotte on their way to Hilton Head. There was a slight chance Melissa would be speaking to him again by Saturday night.

Melissa came in with a bag of groceries and said hello to him before she started putting food away. It was the sort of hello you'd give a panhandler on the sidewalk.

Rich walked over to put his plate in the dishwasher. "I was only teasing with you earlier."

Melissa continued to place vegetables in the refrigerator bins.

"You know, what I said about Thomas. I was joking."

"It didn't sound like teasing to me."

"What did it sound like?"

"Like you thought, number one, that I would be interested in some former Miss-North-Carolina-dating, Viper-driving, superficial man like J. Thomas Sewell.

And, number two, like the only reason he would be interested in me was because of my agency accounts or in case I desperately needed a sperm donor."

Rich put his arms around her. "I said all that. I could have sworn I just made a little joke. Besides, I'm tired of that guy hanging around. He's like a moose in mating season or something."

"Well, it's your problem. And I don't know why, if you're having a territorial problem with Thomas, you have to put me in the middle. I know you've got a lot going on, but the rest of us are not sitting around eating bon-bons and doing our nails."

"I know that. Don't let it upset you so much. It was an innocent joke, and I'm sorry."

Melissa's face softened slightly and she put her hand to her ear, "Did I hear the 'S' word?"

"I'm sorry."

"Apology accepted." She kissed him. "I love you."

"Do we have time to kiss and make up before Andrew gets home?"

Before she could answer, there was the sound of a car in the driveway and Andrew's voice shouting good-bye.

Rich sighed as Melissa moved to finish putting away the groceries. "It starts when they're infants and it never ends. They have some kind of sixth sense."

Melissa winked at him from across the kitchen. They heard Andrew's gym bag drop in the laundry room. He walked in, his hair still wet from his post-game shower.

"I'm starving, Mom. What's to eat?"

"There's chicken and a salad in the refrigerator. I'll get you a plate to heat the chicken on." Melissa gave Andrew a peck on the cheek as she walked by. "You played well tonight, honey."

"Thanks Mom, but that number twenty-one should have never beat me like that. Twice in a row, too."

Rich shook his head. "You've got to move your feet. Your flying angel move gives him a wide open lane to the basket."

"I know, Dad. But if I played him tight he would do that darn spin move."

"There are four other guys out there with you. You've got to work as a team."

Melissa handed Andrew the plate, but looked at Rich as she spoke. "We all make mistakes now and then. Hopefully, we learn from them."

Bright and early Saturday morning, Rich sat down and worked on the charter for the Whitehead Team.

By ten, he was done and he took a minute to review some routine correspondence from the office. He and Andrew had decided to go to the gym at eleven. If Rich got on with it, he could lift weights before they went. There was a set in the basement that Andrew worked out with regularly. Why was it that you only had time for things like that when you were young enough to have toned muscles regardless of what you did or didn't do? Since the merger with Stabler, even Melissa and Kelly used the weights more often than Rich did.

In the basement, it was slow going. With every repetition he did, Rich's muscles reminded him how long it had been since they had put forth this sort of effort. He and Melissa had set aside some time this afternoon to review the proposal from Sewell & Prather. Rich knew the baby discussion was going to come up again. He felt like saying, "Been there, done that." But he knew Melissa wouldn't let it go that easily. Rich counted reps under his breath.

Twelve. Maybe the Sewell & Prather deal won't go through. That would clear up this baby thing. Thirteen. Melissa wouldn't possibly have time for a baby if she was still running an agency. You wish. She's not going to let go of this thing until we work it out one way or the other. Fourteen. Man, I've lost arm strength. These weights feel like they weigh a hundred pounds a piece.

One. What the hell is going on with Walter anyway? Does he just enjoy screwing up people's lives? Two. Can he be that incompetent or does he have something personal against me? Three. The Whitehead account—of all accounts to be jacking around with—what was the deal with that?

Four. Maybe Walter figured that would be the account his Dad would hear from first. I've got to contain Walter. He's like the Ebola virus. Five. Once he's out there, who can say where he will strike next? Six.

"Cool, Dad. You're finally going to start lifting again." Andrew walked down the basement steps with a basketball under his arm, interrupting both Rich's count and his thoughts.

"One session does not a habit make, but I'm determined to get back to some sort of routine. Ready to go?"

"Whenever. I'll be out in the driveway shooting."

"Let me slip on my sweat pants and change my shoes, and I'll be right out to meet you."

At the gym, Rich and Andrew used one basket to play half-court. They were joined by several of Andrew's friends and Jake, who Rich knew was working up an appetite so he could come raid the Morrison refrigerator. A small army ate less than Andrew and Jake combined. They recruited a couple of players using the other half of the court and a full-court pick-up game began.

"Only two rules. No hard fouls, and take it easy on the old guy," Rich instructed the other nine guys before they started.

Andrew captained one team, Jake the other. Rich noticed that one of Andrew's teammates quickly established himself as a shooter. Two other guys might have great looks at the basket, but 'Pistol Pete' never felt the need to throw it their way. After three plays that ran exactly that way and ended with the ball clanging off the rim, his teammates huddled and let loose.

"Man, are you crazy? Pass the ball. I'm open."

"No kidding."

"You keep bricking like that and we're toast."

Andrew chided 'Pete.' "Give up the ball. They've figured out the 'dribble down and heave it up' play. If you pass they'll be so shocked, we're sure to score. Try it a couple of times. If you confuse them with a pass, you may actually get a good look at the basket."

Rich breathed deep and tried to slow his heart rate back into the normal range. He listened to Andrew and his teammates. Well, he thought, they are past forming and right on into storming. No more 'I'll hold back and wait to see what happens.' Everybody was in there pitching for himself.

The next two times down the court, Andrew's team scored. 'Pistol Pete' was left out of the loop. On the third time down, 'Pistol Pete' stood wide open at the top of the key. He waved his hand in the direction of the ballhandler. The player dribbled the ball, ignored him, and passed the ball into the middle of the lane. Jake picked off the pass and scored for his team.

Andrew motioned for his team to huddle.

"Bad pass, you had an open man."

The passer grumbled, "He didn't pass to me when I had a shot."

"Come on guys. They've got the height. We've got the speed. If we don't hit the open guy, we're not going to get back in this. Give the open man the ball. It's like whine or win."

The next trip down the floor, the same thing happened. 'Pistol Pete' was wide open. The guy bringing the ball down the court looked in 'Pete's' direction and hesitated. 'Pete's' defender dropped off Rich, who he had double-teamed, and covered Pete. Another missed shot.

Andrew called for a huddle. "Man, you guys cannot keep ignoring the guy who's wide open. Do you want to win this game or do you want to keep trying to play one on five?"

Definitely still storming, Rich thought.

After the huddle, Rich shot a hook from the right side of the lane that bounced off the rim. Andrew came down with the rebound, passed the ball to 'Pistol Pete' who drove around his defender and scored. Then 'Pistol Pete' picked off a cross-court pass and dished off to the man behind him to set up an easy lay-up. His teammates congratulated him.

On to the real work and norming, Rich thought.

If only he could get Irving and George integrated that well into the Leadership Team. George, in particular, was convinced he had to score every point made. Meanwhile, his teammates were mad. Not only could they not score, they were losing, and George seemed concerned only for himself.

Andrew's team pulled out a come-from-behind win by a basket.

Rich showered quickly when they returned home. Going down the hall to his office, he pulled the proposal from his briefcase on his desk. The offer from Sewell & Prather looked good. It gave Melissa money up front as well as stock in Sewell & Prather.

Melissa poked her head through the doorway. "I'll be with you in one more minute. I've got to get cleaned up."

After a morning at the other desk in the office, with her head stuck in agency accounts, Melissa had gone shopping with Kelly for a dress to wear to the winter dance at school. When they returned, Kelly went off to a friend's house to work on a science project. Melissa, on the other hand, worked out all her frustrations by planting pansies in the yard, digging in the dirt with a gusto that shopping with a seventeen-year-old brings out.

When she returned in clean jeans and a long-sleeved T-shirt, Rich asked, "Did you find a dress?"

"We did. We compromised somewhere between the dress I liked, which she thought looked like something her grandmother would wear, and the one she liked, which I thought looked like something a call girl would wear, an expensive call girl mind you, but still a call girl."

Melissa sat down in the chair across the desk from Rich. Her jade shirt stood out against the neutral beige coloring of the office they shared.

"Do you realize that this is the first Saturday that we've had any time to call our own since Christmas?"

Rich hoped it wouldn't be the last one until next Christmas. "I know, and with this project at Stabler I don't have a clue what my schedule is going to be like except crazy."

Rich picked up the proposal from Sewell & Prather. "This looks like a pretty decent offer. Is there a catch I'm missing?"

"None, except working for someone else. I actually thought the offer was a little low myself."

"I guess some of that depends on how they arrived at the value of their stock. What do you think it should be?"

"At least fifty thousand more in cash. I don't want stock. Especially since I don't want to work for them anyway. Baby or no baby, I can't see myself going back to that life."

"Well, let's suppose, and I'm not saying that we've made that decision. Just suppose that we decide against having another child. What do you think you'd like to do?"

"Something completely different. A Ph.D. in French Literature."

"That's marketable. We hired two of those guys last week."

Melissa flicked his arm with her hand. "Very funny. I didn't say I wanted to be practical. If the agency sells for enough, I can finish off the children's college funds and then play. Maybe I'll paint, maybe I'll write. Maybe I'll study Aboriginal tribes."

"The commute time on that would be a killer."

"Okay, smart aleck. The point is, the sale of AdWorks was meant to be. I've been a little restless lately anyway."

"I had no idea. This baby thing hit me like a bolt out of the blue."

"Maybe that's what it took for me to get your full attention. Of course, you had no idea. Stabler has consumed you."

"Now that's not fair, I'm doing the best I can."

"I didn't say I was being fair. But if I paid attention like you have been in the past few months, where do you think the kids would be? In juvenile court or worse."

Rich felt attacked. "So why would we want to bring one more baby into the world to be incarcerated? I'm confused."

"So am I. You'd think after nineteen years—"

Melissa's voice broke.

Rich realized how frustrated she was. He reached over and took her hand. "Okay. Time out. Let's do one issue at a time. First, we'll discuss this proposal and then we can talk about what you'd like to do next. If the sale goes through, that is."

The phone rang. When it made it through a second complete ring, Rich knew Kelly and Andrew were out of the house. The voice on the other end was Patty Mitchell, with whom they were supposed to have dinner in a few hours.

"Rich, hey, I'm glad I caught you at home. We're going to have to do a raincheck on dinner tonight."

"You're not going to Hilton Head?" Rich asked.

"No, David's come down with a bad case of the flu and we just don't feel comfortable leaving today. Mark's parents were coming to stay with the boys, but they are getting too old to expose them to this sort of thing. Sorry it's such short notice. Anyway, maybe next time."

"Oh sure, no problem. Hope David gets to feeling better." Rich motioned with his hand so that Melissa would know it was nothing serious.

"I'm sure he'll be fine. Mark and I were looking forward to this as an early anniversary trip, but that's life. It sure doesn't seem like nineteen years. Time flies. Maybe we can all celebrate next year with a cruise. Anyway, you two go on and have a great anniversary dinner anyway."

That was it. No wonder Melissa was so unhappy. It was their anniversary today. Nineteen years ago, he and Melissa had barely been married a month when Mark and Patty had eloped. Rich couldn't believe he'd forgotten his wedding anniversary.

Rich hung up the phone with Patty. "David's got the flu and Mark's parents were supposed to come and stay with the boys." Should he acknowledge the anniversary now or wait and try to fix it another way?

Melissa looked concerned. "How sick is he?"

"Patty says he'll be fine, they just don't want to expose Mark's parents."

"I hate that. I was looking forward to seeing Mark and Patty."

Rich looked at the clock. The jewelry store at the mall should still be open. What about the roses? Every anniversary, he sent Melissa one rose for every year of their marriage. If he worked fast, maybe he could get them delivered over to the restaurant and surprise her.

"Rich, are you okay?" Melissa waved her hand back and forth in front of his eyes. "Come back, wherever you are."

"Sure, I'm fine. There's no reason why you and I can't still go and enjoy dinner together. I'll just change the reservation at the Lamplighter for two."

"Whatever." Melissa shrugged her shoulders.

"Tell you what, honey, let's talk about this proposal later. Think about what you want to counter with. Did I mention that I promised Andrew that we'd go look for some new basketball shoes?"

"I thought Andrew was at Chad's house. And besides, he got new shoes at the beginning of the season. Don't tell me that his shoes are not going to last a whole season anymore." Melissa frowned. "Are you sure you're okay?"

Rich shoved papers into a folder and avoided Melissa's eyes. "Just fine. Andrew is into some serious playing now. You don't want him to get hurt because he's wearing some old shoes. I told him earlier I'd pick him up at Chad's."

As soon as Rich was in the Suburban, he called Chad's house and talked to Andrew. "Don't ask questions, I'll be by to pick you up in ten minutes. Chad too, if he wants to go to the mall. If your mother calls, tell her we're going to go look for some new shoes for you and that we planned it this morning. Got it?"

"Sure Dad, anything you say."

Andrew hung up the phone and made a face at Chad.

"Parents. Who can figure them out?"

GOOSE CHASE

"To paraphrase Joan Crawford, 'Change is fire, but whether it's going to warm you up or burn down your house remains to be seen.' If I were you, I'd keep the fire department's number handy."

— Melissa Morrison to her husband, Rich, after a romantic dinner for two at the Lamplighter

CHAPTER EIGHT

"You can lead a horse to water, but you can't make him drink," Rich's father said.

"But you can feed that horse salt and make him thirsty," his grandfather replied.

The two men held an open discussion in Rich's head as he sat in bumper-to-bumper traffic on Monday morning. He inched the Suburban along and thought how true his father's favorite saying was. Changing someone else was impossible. On the other hand, his grandfather was right. You could motivate them. Still, they had to change themselves.

How could he motivate people? So many 'change' programs had come and gone. There was no doubt Stabler excelled at starting change—follow-through was another story.

He popped the button on his radio and pounding music blared around him. "BABY, YOU MAKE MY STOMACH TURN, I'M YOUR ROMEO, YOU'RE MY JULIET." He turned the volume down and hit the select button for 104.2. Kelly had taken the Suburban Sunday night to pick up some milk. It's no wonder she doesn't hear half of what you say, Rich thought. She's deaf.

Sort of like Stabler's employees, the word 'change' had been shouted at them so much they were deaf to it. It hardly registered with them, and if it did, their eyes did that glaze-over thing and they started to look like extras from "Night of the Living Dead." Some of the Kinton employees still referred to the DC as Kinton instead of Stabler.

Marketing was never this way. Sure, you had your flakes, but being innovative kept your job for you and people knew it. Ahead, the stoplight turned red and traffic crept to a halt. Behind him some guy in a Mercedes was trying to fight his way into the left-hand lane so he could be the sixth car at the stoplight instead of the seventh.

"The aroma leaves you wanting more. We roast all our beans on-site. Classic Carolina Coffees. Experience that international flavor, right here in Charlotte. Visit us at Southpark Mall or at our web site—www.caro.java.com."

Rich pulled his coffee mug out of its holder and took a sip. Maybe he should make a commercial for 'change.' "Visit us at our web site—www.do it or die.com." Rich laughed out loud at the thought, jostling his coffee which just missed sloshing over the edge of the mug. He carefully placed the mug back in its holder. His grandfather's voice pushed his way back into Rich's thoughts. "I never made anyone buy a box of Corn Toasties. I made them think about Corn Toasties, and when the time to buy came they'd thought about them enough to choose them."

A commercial might not be so dumb after all. Rich smiled to himself as he began to think of 'change' commercials. He tapped the steering wheel in time to the radio commercial's jingle. He couldn't wait to tell the team. Imagine what Bob Ketchum's face would look like. Rich laughed out loud as the light changed to green. He realized that a couple of people in a mini-van next to him were staring. They turned their heads to him when he looked over. Nevertheless, he grinned all the way to the office, feeling slightly maniacal.

Barbara picked up on his good mood. "Good weekend?"

"Great weekend. I think I've got something," he said.

"I hope the rest of us don't catch it," she laughed.

"I'm going to do my best to infect everyone."

"Well, I'll warn Valerie Wagner then. She's already called and wants to see you as soon as you can get to her," Barbara said.

"Great. Conference call with Boston is at ten, right?" Rich asked.

"That's right. Are you going to want to use the conference room for that?"

"I'll take it in my office. Please check with Irving Steed to see if he can make it over for that," Rich said.

"Will do," Barbara answered, already reaching for the phone.

Rich walked into his office and rang Valerie's extension. Ten minutes later she walked in, knocking lightly on Rich's door as she entered. A tall woman, Valerie commanded attention simply by walking in a room. She always wore very plain business suits. They were tailored, almost prim looking. Her personal trademarks were the large silver pins and big silver earrings that she wore with them. Valerie's husband was in the import-export business and Rich overheard Barbara comment that she rarely saw Valerie wear the same pin twice. Today's pin was a big star with one of the bottom points extending well below the others. Her hair style was as consistent as her suits; she wore it swept back away from her face. Rich ran into Valerie one Saturday in the garden store and had to take a second look to recognize her with her blonde hair down across her shoulders.

"You want the bad news or the good news first?" Valerie asked.

Rich motioned her to a seat before he clasped his hands behind his head and said, "I'm not into delayed gratification this morning. Give me the good news first."

"The good news is there's a lot happening in the Quality Team meetings," Valerie said.

"And the bad?" Rich asked.

"None of it is getting them out of the storming cycle. From what I can gather, George Nader is driving them crazy. Quality is holding up shipments and then George refuses to discuss a different way of doing the checking. It's as if the charter for the Quality Team reads, 'Improve quality inspections, but don't change the procedures or the system.' Not too hard to figure out why people are frustrated. When I asked team members about it, I got a lot of people muttering under their breath. And the names they're calling George are not ones you want to give your first-born," Valerie said.

"How do you think we fix it?"

"Aside from inundating George with subliminal teaming messages? I think first of all we need to go back and rework the team charter. It might be that we need to add someone else from the Leadership Team to assist George. Get him to back off a bit so the team can start to move into the norming phase. I honestly don't know what will work. And we don't have much time to tinker.

"Another thing. George acts so secretive about information. Kind of like quality is 'Mission Impossible' and people only get information on George's idea of a need-to-know basis. It's really turning people off. If all his energy could be redirected into a 'we' mentality, he could rule the world."

"My granddaddy was fond of saying, 'If a toad had wings, he wouldn't bump his ass on the ground,'"Rich said.

Rich worried that George would be forever stuck in 'us vs. them' which ultimately meant 'us' and 'them' would both lose.

"What if I told you that I think we may not need a quality department?" Rich asked.

"I'd tell you that I'm not going to mention that to George. And if you are planning on mentioning it to George, I'd like to put in my request for time off right now," Valerie said.

"Seriously. If we leave quality totally in the hands of production. Then what?" Rich asked.

"This isn't really my area, Rich. But what about stuff we're getting from overseas?" She asked.

"I don't know the details, but it could be that what our Quality Team needs to be doing is figuring out how not to have a quality department."

"That sounds great on paper, but people aren't going to come up with the solution that axes their jobs, do you think?" Valerie sounded skeptical.

"They would if they see there might be a new position. Working with the plants and suppliers to be sure what we're getting is quality. You, George and I need to meet on that and get a new charter worked out ASAP. Do you have time this afternoon?"

"I do. I'll check with George. Then I'm going to go buy a big bottle of Maalox."

Rich laughed. "Call me as soon as you know something." Rich made himself a note on the charter.

"The other thing I needed to mention ..." Valerie hesitated.

Rich looked up from his notepad, giving her his full attention.

"Lisa Perkins, from corporate, is calling me about training. She insists that we put together some training programs for everyone. Walter's direct order. I tried to explain our 'just-in-time' training approach and either she doesn't get it or Walter won't let her get it. Do I stall or go at it again?"

Rich sighed, "I'll put it on my list of Walter issues. Chances are that Lisa's been told this is a mandatory thing."

"It would probably be helpful in the long run if we educated the corporate people involved," Valerie said.

"That's not a bad suggestion. Why don't you add it to the Leadership Team agenda. I've been thinking about this whole change thing. Tell me, what would we do if we were trying to sell a product?"

"Advertise," Valerie said tentatively.

"Exactly," Rich replied. "So why wouldn't we advertise to sell change? To get past people's resistance. A commercial or two."

"I suppose that would work." Valerie's enthusiasm seemed doubtful.

"What's wrong with it?" Rich asked.

"Nothing. I think it's great to start with, but it seems to me that we're better at adopting slogans and printing T-shirts than we are at helping people know how to change."

"So what do you think we need?"

"I think the commercials are a great idea. Do something beyond slogans that people aren't expecting. I wonder if we don't need to develop something that will help people see how they can overcome their anxieties and get on board the new company. A sort of personal path forward that meshes with the forward path of the company. Not training. More, here's what you need to think about and some information on how to get there."

"Okay." Rich worked at overcoming his disappointment that Valerie didn't have his level of enthusiasm for commercials. He tried to focus on her point. "Can you give me a for instance?"

"Suppose we do decide to abolish quality and those people are moved into new positions. Maybe positions we haven't even had before. They need something to help them see how they are going to get there. Tools to work with."

"But we can't coddle people. It won't work. Those that are independent resent it and those that aren't independent grow more dependent on someone else doing it for them," Rich said.

Valerie shook her head. "I don't mean coddle them. Give them a chance to change. You and I both know we can't change anybody. They've got to change themselves."

"Exactly," Rich said. "It looks like you may have worked yourself into another assignment. Put that on the Leadership Team's agenda. Now what about the other teams?"

"The Garment on Hanger (GOH) Team is working pretty well. They've actually offered two suggestions that cut the time it takes to get the garments on hangers by about twenty percent. It shouldn't be long before they've fulfilled their charter and are ready to disband.

"The Communication Team may be ready for an oil change. They've been together longer than anyone else besides the Leadership Team, and Rachel Alvarado thinks they may be ready for some new blood."

Rachel Alvarado was the Communication Team's liaison.

"I've gotten everyone's agenda items for Tuesday's Leadership Team meeting. I'll just need to add commercials and tools."

Rich's intercom buzzed.

"Walter's on line one. You want to call him back?" Barbara said.

"Hang on. Anything else?" Rich asked Valerie.

Valerie shook her head.

"I'll take it, Barbara," Rich said.

Valerie waved on her way out the door.

Rich talked to Walter about the Whitehead Team. Then he explained the logic of 'just-in-time' training to Walter, who acted as if he had never mentioned the subject before.

"I'll talk to you about it some more when I see you, but just ask Lisa to back off a bit, if you would, please."

"No problem, Rich."

Bob Ketchum came in and Rich motioned him to take a seat. Rich noticed that Bob's coloring looked better, the gray-green of a week ago was replaced by a shade of white that would almost pass for healthy.

"I'll have Barbara fax you all the charters for the teams and the personnel on each one. Let me know if you have any questions," Rich said, winding up his conversation with Walter.

Bob sat down, his ample frame obscuring a large portion of the gray chair.

"Okay, Bob, tell me where we have the greatest bottleneck. What creates the greatest delays in the shipping area?" Rich had his thoughts, but he wanted to hear Bob's ideas.

"Quality wins by a landslide. George's people have to get their hands in everything." Bob held up his hand as if he anticipated what George would say to that statement. "Which I know—the customer needs the right shipment. But George has checkers going back and inspecting fabric—fabric that has already passed one quality inspection in manufacturing. They look at it like they're going to find flaws in every piece. Give me a break. If the fabric was good to start with—get over it and get the stuff out of here. Hell, you'd think they're getting paid by the piece."

Rich knew they weren't getting paid by the piece, but he also knew that performance of the quality department was measured by the number of pieces inspected. That explained somewhat the quality personnel's need to have their fingers in every box.

"Do you know how much they actually end up pulling?" Rich asked.

"Not for sure, but it seems like, oh, every million orders or so, they find a mistake. Meanwhile, the stuff is waiting to be shipped while I've got customer service people and sales reps jumping up and down. Standing on their heads cause they were promised the stuff yesterday."

"I just spoke to Valerie. The Quality Team needs a jump start. It could be that we need to rethink the whole quality issue," Rich said.

Bob got up and walked to the door. "That discussion ought to be interesting. One more thing, Rich. I'd like to be on that Whitehead Team if you think it makes sense."

It surprised Rich to hear Bob volunteer.

"Glad to hear that, Bob. You're already on my list."

Bob's bulky frame filled the doorway. "Yeah, I knew you'd figure somebody had to help those jack-legs keep their heads screwed on straight."

"That's the team attitude," Rich deadpanned.

Bob saluted and left without saying anything else.

Barbara buzzed him again. "Carlos Burns is on line one."

Carlos Burns was the manager of one of Stabler's new distribution centers. Located in Miami, Carlos was actually employed by the third-party firm that ran the entire Miami operation for one of the companies that Donald had acquired.

"Rich, have you heard any more news on what's going to happen with our contract?" Carlos asked.

"Carlos, today you probably know more than I do about what's going on. I've just gotten the word up here that we're going to completely redesign our systems. Looks like we'll start with the Charlotte operation. Donald is taking the position that we're under siege, so a decision on your long-term status is a ways off. In the short-term, just keep on doing what you're doing. That doesn't give you a lot to go on, but you know we would honor all the terms of the notice that we originally agreed to with your people."

"Rich, why don't you let me look at some of your redesign? Maybe we could help you with what you're doing. Our system reaches across the country."

"When we get to that point, I'll be happy to talk to you, Carlos. You know the benefits of your system a lot more than I do."

Before the conference call, Rich called John O'Connor in manufacturing. "Quick question for you, John. All your material still goes through a quality inspection, doesn't it?"

"Sure. Before manufacturing, we do a complete material inspection. If it's not top-of-the-line, your guys never see it."

As Rich suspected, the DC's quality inspections duplicated manufacturing's efforts. George wasn't going to like it, but his part of the process was due for an overhaul.

Irving Steed made it into Rich's office just as the conference call began. Larry and Denise in one Boston office and Walter in another hooked into Rich in Charlotte and John O'Connor in Lexington.

The "good mornings" were barely out of everyone's mouth before Walter started in on proprietary information.

"Walter, Denise and I have got a lot to do. Let me assure you that the system we put in place will not allow your average Joe to read the latest payroll list. We are talking about a system that will allow people access to the information we want them to have. Let's face it, Walter, if a hacker wanted to break into our system, they could."

"You're kidding me."

"The good news, Walter, is that there are very few computer geeks out there who have an interest in Stabler's computer files. Surprising as that may be," Larry said.

Rich tried to get back on track. "Look guys, I'm under the gun here on this redesign. So let's get right to the point. How long to get the system up and running and how much is it going to cost?"

"Four months and the ROI comes out to eighteen percent."

"That ROI doesn't sound all that great to me." Walter's voice added an erotic tone to the conference. He said ROI in the same way a redneck says "red hot mama."

"Walter, we've got to do something. If we only look at the short-term, we are going to be short-term. That's not consistent with the Stabler vision, do you think?" Rich shot back. He didn't want anything to dampen Larry Adams' enthusiasm. Adams could get tight with the money when he got into his bean-counter mode and Rich knew he didn't want that to happen.

"No. But I still wish it had a better ROI."

Rich directed his next question to Larry and Denise. "Four months. You're sure you can have this thing rolling in four months?"

"Rich," Denise sounded peeved. "We can do four months. The fact is, I've been trying to get someone to get started on this system for months now. We've been so busy adding new companies, no one was interested in what I had to say."

"This system will let us look at our vendor's performance, their product quality and on-time shipping rate, right?" Rich asked.

"That's right. You could track them down to what their cafeteria served for lunch that day if you wanted to," Denise said.

Everyone laughed.

"Okay, Denise," Rich said. "But I've got Irving Steed here and he's had some problems getting support on the software he needs for the MOD Act. You know—the new customs law. What are we going to do about that?"

"If Irving gets me all his information, we should be able to handle it. Unless it's real unusual, it could probably be networked into this system we're talking about installing."

Irving spoke up. "I sent Reece Pasquale the information months ago."

"Well, I've never seen it. I'll get with Reece and get back to you by the end of the day," Denise said.

"I tell you what—Irving will fax you the information again. That saves you the time looking for it. Then I'll need a proposal from you by tomorrow morning with all the pertinent information and justifications that Donald and, of course, you too, Walter, will need to see."

"I'm light-years ahead of you. I can fax you that information right now." Denise said.

Rich bit his tongue. Sometimes the attitude of the information technology people would lead you to believe they held the secret to life, rather than just a computer program.

John O'Connor spoke up. "I'd like to see the same thing so we can start figuring out how the system will work for us over in the plant."

"I'll fax you a copy, too."

"Can you do that today with Irving's information added in?" Rich asked.

Valerie sounded peeved. "If you get me the information this morning I'll look at it and we'll see what we can do, as long as Larry approves."

"Fine with me. And while you're at it, find out what Reece did with the stuff Irving sent. Those customs fines are nothing to sneeze at." Larry didn't sound happy at the prospect of lost faxes that resulted in government penalties.

"And I can expect full on-site support here in Charlotte until this thing flies?" Rich knew that Valerie preferred phone support, but this project was too massive for that.

"I'll add a hand holder into the budget right now," Denise said.

"Better make that two, Denise, unless you think Rich's people and my folks can share one," John added.

"Denise, make sure I get a copy of that proposal too. I'm going to leave you to work out the details, I'm late for an appointment." Walter tried to sound important. Probably the dentist, Rich thought.

Larry broke in, "Walter, have you had a chance to talk to Donald about those new DCs yet?"

"No, and I've got to run." Walter's line clicked off.

"What new DCs?" Rich asked.

"Actually we were thinking that it makes sense to close some of these DCs we've purchased all over the continent," Larry said.

"Larry, before we get into that I've got to see where we stand right now," Rich said.

"I know, but we could save a bundle if we go ahead and close them down," Larry said.

"That's true," Rich agreed. "But we'll also spend a bundle and more if we have to open them back up. Let's take it one step at a time."

When the call was over, Irving stood to leave.

"Okay, Irving, I'm calling in my chips. I believe your exact words were, 'if you get me some help with customs, I'll help with the redesign.' Are you ready to become a business system guru?" Rich asked.

"I'm a man of my word, Rich. I'm going to go fax that customs information to Denise right now and see what happens."

The rest of the afternoon passed in a parade of phone calls and visitors. Rich had hoped for some time to walk around, but he didn't even get out onto the floor of the DC.

At four-thirty, George and Valerie arrived together. As they sat down, George started, "I told you this team thing wasn't going to work. People don't understand the quality process."

"Why not?" Rich asked.

"Because they keep making suggestions that would weaken our efforts. Nothing goes out of here that isn't one hundred percent right. Product one hundred percent perfect and order correct."

"That's true, George. However, the problem is that the delays we're experiencing in the quality process are impacting our ship dates. Not by hours. Not by a day. But by days, by weeks, and in some cases by the month. I think you're right – the Quality Team isn't working," Rich said.

George seemed surprised at Rich's agreement. "So are we going to abolish the team?"

"No, I think we may abolish the quality department."

"You'd think that these people could make up their minds. Ship, don't ship. It changes from minute to minute. If you're driving for this company, you've got to be a trucker and a member of the psychic network."

— Judy Laney to Bronson Galang, her
  fellow trucker on the Stabler loading
  dock, Charlotte, February

CHAPTER NINE

"What? What did you say?" George laughed like someone who didn't quite get the joke but refused to admit it.

"I said, maybe the mission of the quality team should be to figure out a way to abolish the quality department," Rich said.

"You're not serious." George turned to Valerie. "He's not serious."

"Well ..." She hesitated.

"You're serious." George sounded like a broken record.

Rich broke into the monologue. "George, whatever we do, we need to look at all the possibilities. Open the discussion up, break the paradigm."

"I notice that it's not your job we're discussing here. How about that paradigm?" George asked.

"Donald Stabler said change it and that's what I intend to do."

"He didn't say make a muck of the whole thing, did he?" George's face reddened.

"No, he didn't," Rich said. "But I think we can make a real difference in our overall operations by looking at the quality system, particularly if we have your help. You're the one closest to it. You can either spend your energy protecting it or you can spend your energy figuring out a whole new way to do it. For instance, what about the ISO 9000 certification?"

"People here couldn't handle ISO 9000," George replied.

"I'm not so sure about that."

When the meeting was over, Rich couldn't say what George was thinking. George seemed to understand that he could not sit still, but his direction remained to be seen.

Tuesday morning, the Leadership Team assembled in the conference room. Bob Ketchum brought in hot Krispy Kreme donuts. With the exception of Valerie, the group swooped down on them like vultures.

As he poured himself a cup of coffee, Rich thought that George and Irving still looked uptight. George's mouth was set in a solid line and Irving worked a rubber band like a set of rosary beads, pausing every now and then to take a bite out of his donut.

At one end of the table, Valerie attempted conversation with George but received one-word answers to all her questions. George mostly stared into his donut like it was a crystal ball capable of telling him the future.

At the other end of the table, Rachel and Bob chatted. Bob needs that donut as much as I do, Rich thought, as he polished off the last of his own.

As the meeting began, Bob was appointed recorder. After Rachel reviewed the Model of Success and the team rules, Rich briefly discussed the last meeting including the action items. Rachel and Bob reported that they had decided on two firms to benchmark. Both were lingerie manufacturers; one specialized in sleepwear and the other produced and distributed a complete line of lingerie. Everyone agreed with Bob that they needed accurate baseline data of their own to compare with these two firms.

Irving reported on the new MRP II program and answered questions about its capabilities. Several people asked questions that required him to check with the IT people at corporate. Irving promised to circulate a memo with those answers.

Rich presented the charter for the Whitehead Team:

CHARTER FOR THE WHITEHEAD SERVICE TEAM
TEAM SPONSOR: Rich Morrison
DATE: February 12, 1995
Leadership Team Preliminary: February 16, 1995
Leadership Team Final: February 23, 1995

| WST Team Review: | February 28, 1995 |
| WST Team Acceptance: | March 14, 1995 |

I. OPPORTUNITY: (What is the reason this team exists?)

The Stabler Leadership Team has identified a need to continuously improve the customer service of one of our critical accounts, the Whitehead chain. This team should assure efficient and effective procedures for defining requirements, complying to all labeling standards, on-time delivery, and accurate order fulfillment. This team's opportunity is to develop a plan to provide a 100% fill rate on the first shipment, on-time delivery and conform to carton labeling and pricing needs while achieving reductions in the cost of distribution.

II. PROCESS: (What are the steps to be followed and what are the questions to be answered by this team?)

The WST (Whitehead Service Team) will follow the Stabler process of team-based continuous improvement as follows:

1. Team orientation
2. Review/Revise/Accept charter
3. Data collection
4. Assess status and develop baseline
5. Define Evidence of Success
6. Prioritize opportunities
7. Brainstorm alternatives
8. Identify improvement plans
9. Evaluate improvement plans
10. Define improvement plans
11. Obtain improvement plan support
12. Implement improvement plan
13. Return to Step 3.

III. EVIDENCE OF SUCCESS: (What results are expected in what time frames for this team to be successful?)

1.   100% fill rate on the first shipment within 9 months
2.   Increase on-time delivery to 95% within 9 months
3.   Comply to all label and pricing requests within 9 months
4.   Develop a procedure for promotions and ticketing for all 300 stores within 6 months
5.   Reduce the total costs of distribution by 20% within 9 months.

IV. RESOURCES: (Who are the team members, team leader and team liaison, who will support the team if needed, how much time should be spent both in meetings and outside of meetings, and what additional resources are available to the team?)

The team will consist of the following people:

Team Members: Israel Stanley – Customer Service
Marcus Warren – Marketing and Sales
Larry Adams – Finance and Information Technology
Denise Burton – Information Technology
John O'Connor – Manufacturing
Bob Ketchum – Distribution
Raymond Rodriquez – Planning

Team Leader: Rich Morrison – Logistics
Team Liaison: Rachel Alvarado – Customer Sevice

The team should meet one hour per week and spend an additional one hour per week in preparation. The team leader should spend a total of three hours per week devoted to the WST.

V. CONSTRAINTS: (What authority does the team have, what is the overall time frame for the evolution of the empowerment process, what things cannot be changed, what items are outside the scope of the team, and what budget does the team have?)

1. The team shall complete its work in 12 months. The team should evolve from a Suggestion Team to an Improvement Team once their Whitehead Action Plan Report is accepted by the Leadership Team.

2. The AMAPS software shall be the base system.

3. The team shall interface with the ongoing Customer Satisfaction and Cost Reduction Teams.

4. Inventory management systems must conform to the corporate standards.

5. No more than $2,000 shall be spent without the approval of Rich Morrison. To spend less than $2,000, account code DIM 4836 shall be used. The total annual budget for DIM 4836 is $4,000.

6. No travel shall be charged to DIM 4836. Any travel shall be done against the individual departments' budgets.

VI. EXPECTATIONS: (What are the outputs from the team? When are they expected to be complete, and to whom should they be given?)

1. The team shall publish weekly minutes.

2. The team shall make a monthly presentation at the Communications Forum.

3. The team shall produce a Whitehead Action Plan Report in two months. This report shall present and justify a recommended path forward.

4. The team shall recommend the creation of an Implementation Team in three months. A draft charter of this new team should be submitted to the Leadership Team.

Rich continued, "From customer service, I think our members should be Israel Stanley and Rachel; from sales and marketing, I think, the team member should be Marcus Warren; from planning, I think, Raymond Rodriquez, and from finance and IT, Larry Adams and Denise Burton. I think Bob should be on the team from distribution and John O'Connor from manufacturing. I'll serve as the team leader and Rachel will be team liaison. Valerie will serve in a special ad-hoc role since we'll need to bring the people from outside the DC up to speed on the teaming process."

"I question whether Marcus is going to be able to effectively work with this team right now. It seems like he has his hands full," Bob said.

"Okay. Do you have someone else in mind?" Rich asked.

"Nandy Gamble would be a good choice. It might help her to see the whole process from start to finish. Raymond is always complaining about the way she paints planning into a corner," Rachel volunteered.

"Good idea. But I still think Marcus needs to be on the team. We've got to have a high level of support from everyone to make this happen."

Valerie reported on the current in-house teams which brought up the issue of quality.

"I've been thinking," Irving said, "Denise Burton told us that this new computer system can profile our vendors. I've talked to George a little bit, and we've come up with a list of quality criteria. If we can track our vendors on carton count accuracy, misships, inbound carton damage, missing labels, on-time shipments, back orders and information completeness, particularly the accuracy of their advanced shipping notices, then we would have a good idea which vendors' shipments we need to check."

"Or what vendors we don't need to be using at all," George added.

"If every box didn't have to be opened, we could do a lot more crossdocking," Bob Ketchum added. "That would reduce operations cost, reduce inventory and increase our capacity."

"Excellent. George and Irving need to explore what it will take to make that happen. Bob, you need to start thinking of who the most likely crossdocking candidates would be," Rich said.

Everyone nodded and Rich was pleased to see George make a note on his pad. This was progress compared to his earlier donut trance.

"Valerie and I have been talking about what we need to bring about change. Greater business gurus than myself have said that companies don't change, the people in them do. My question was, how do we motivate and encourage people to change? I think people need to see that we are serious about follow-through this time. I also think that Donald Stabler and our executive committee have given us wide parameters to work within, actually, close to no parameters at all. At the same time, I feel that they need to be educated in the process of teaming. Valerie has pointed out to me that just-in-time training is another area where our approach needs to be explained.

"One of the ways I think we can do that is to run a 'change' campaign. Weave the fabric of change into everyone's thought processes. Maybe some commercials or a series of famous change agents or people who didn't change when they should have. For example, a poster of Marie Antoinette saying, 'Perhaps I shouldn't have used the word cake.'"

Rich turned to Rachel. "Rachel, the Communication Team needs to be brought up to speed on what we're doing so that they can get the message out."

"I'll put it on this week's agenda," Rachel said.

"Now, I also want Valerie to share with you what she sees as imperative to the new Stabler," Rich said.

"As I mentioned to Rich, people need more than motivation, they need tools. For instance, with personal changes such as weight loss—can a weight loss program make someone lose weight?" Valerie said.

Bob interrupted, "Could you use another example besides weight loss?" He took his hand and tried to shield his donut from the group.

Everyone laughed.

Valerie continued, "The answer is no. A weight loss program cannot make anyone lose weight. The person must be motivated to lose weight. The weight loss program simply provides them with the tools and then rewards them with a new physique when they're done. I feel like we need to give people as many tools as possible. Information that will help them chart their own path forward in our company."

"So is this some sort of training that you think we all need?" Rachel asked.

"No. I don't consider it training. Helping to develop a real sense of power over the choices everyone will be called on to make. Jobs may change. People around them may change. What will they do to take charge of all that?"

More discussion followed and the meeting ended with the review of action items assigned. Rich would continue to work on getting approval for the Whitehead Service Team. George and Irving were to explore the software capabilities needed to make crossdocking happen. Irving needed to get answers to other software questions the group had. Rachel and the Communication Team would continue to work on other ways to get the word out about change. Bob and Rachel would complete the benchmarking process and get some baseline data from Warehouse Information Systems.

The intercom buzzed and Rich picked up the conference room phone. Barbara's voice had a hint of exasperation in it. "Marcus Warren is on line one and he insists on talking to you now. Some crisis with the Rollins stores."

"Okay, I'll pick it up." Rich put his hand over the receiver. "Thanks for coming everyone. We've got a good start. I'm going to Boston Thursday so let's plan to meet Friday at noon. We'll order in lunch if everyone can make it then."

"Now if we only knew where we were going," George muttered as he left the room.

Rich pushed a button on the phone. "Marcus, what's going on?"

"Rich, you have got to do something about your screw-ups in Charlotte. The Rollins stores have been running a promotional ad, *Buy Stabler's A Slim-Me, get a lingerie bag and a sample of Woolens delicate wash free*, in four major southeastern cities. Rollins asked us to ship the product with the bags attached. One day before their order is supposed to ship, I get a message from Bob Ketchum that it won't be going out. The penalties will kill us, IF we don't lose the account altogether. We messed up the tags on the *Buy three, Get one free* promotion at Rollins not three months ago."

"Hold on a second, Marcus, I don't know anything about this. What's the ship date?" Rich asked.

"Tomorrow is, but I've built in an extra two days into the schedule like I always do. We'd never ship anything on time if I didn't. So we actually have until Friday," Marcus said.

"Let me get with Bob Ketchum and find out what's going on. I'll get back to you before the end of the day," Rich said.

Rich walked down the hall to Bob's office. Stacks of paper covered every inch of Bob's desk. On the right edge, Rich noticed a pile that leaned toward the window, almost as if it was growing to the sun. Rich moved a stack of trade magazines off a chair and sat down.

"I just got off the phone with Marcus Warren. The steam coming out of the phone damned near burned my ear off. What's the problem with the Rollins promotional merchandise?" Rich said.

Bob leaned back in his chair and put his hands behind his head.

"The problem is just what I told him the problem would be four months ago when he promised them this crap. The vendor who supplies the lingerie bags makes our ship schedule look world-class. I've been on the phone with the little weasels for two weeks. Every day they're promising to ship. I've got the girdles all ready to go and I finally get the bags today so we can shrink wrap them with the girdles, and they're wrong."

Rich felt a kink begin to form in his neck. "What do you mean they're wrong? How can you tell?"

"Because lingerie bags are supposed to have little holes in them, so when they're in the wash all the water can run out like those colander thingies that you rinse spaghetti in. These bags—no holes—solid vinyl. They're something like a woman would carry in her purse to put her lipstick in or something. The samples were supposed to be packed inside. No Woolen samples, wrong bags. I'm not a miracle worker, Rich."

Bob straightened his arms up over his head with the palms up.

"So where are the samples supposed to be coming from?" Rich rubbed the tight spot in his neck.

"Out of Atlanta."

"Have you checked with the supplier to see when he can get you the right bags?" Rich asked.

Bob laughed. "Yeah, right before hell freezes over. He says day after tomorrow, but I think that's right up there with the check's in the mail and I'm here from corporate to help you."

"Well, that's not going to do us any good, anyway," Rich said.

"Let Marcus Warren, 'Mr. World Class Marketing,' find some bags." Bob leaned forward in his chair and put his hands on his desk. His knuckles were white from the pressure his fingers exerted on the surface. "He knows it all."

"So these are his suppliers that you're dealing with?"

"That's right. His people set it all up. I'm just the shrink wrap man. And at the rate we're going I'm going to need a damn shrink."

"How fast could you turn the shipment around if you had the right stuff?" Rich asked.

Bob thought about it for a minute. "Thirty-six hours."

"How about twenty-four?"

"Yeah, sure. And then I'll go part the Red Sea when I'm finished. Just make sure Marcus Warren and his bunch are in the middle of it when I let go." Bob smirked.

"I mean it, Bob. If we put everyone on it, could we do it in twenty-four hours?"

"I suppose it's possible, if the wrapping machinery holds up. But then that will throw everything else behind. And that behind stuff will include a great big Whitehead order."

"Well, we'll have to work out something. I want to see a ship list for everything that needs to go out between now and Friday. Start figuring out how you can get these promos out of here. Is there any way we can use the DC in Miami to take some of the load?" Rich asked.

"Search me. I guess it depends on how many of these girdles they have down there in Miami and whether the promo supplier can ship the giveaways to them as quick as they can to us."

Rich wondered if the proposed computer system would allow them quick access to that sort of information. "Wonder how we find that out?" Rich stood and moved towards the door.

"Try a magic eight ball. Where are you going now?" Bob asked.

"I'm going to go call Marcus Warren. He needs to get us those bags and samples if he wants us to get this order out of here."

"I'll get you the ship list, but you've got to let me know if it's a go so I can rework the schedule," Bob said.

"Will do. And, Bob, one more thing. Nobody calls them girdles anymore, the correct term is for our product is A Slim-Me. *Slimmies*, if you prefer."

Rich could hear Bob muttering as he walked away. "A girdle's a girdle."

Darla rolled her eyes at Rich as he passed her desk. "I've tried and tried to tell him that. He says we're lucky he's quit calling underwear, bloomers. You can't teach an old dog new tricks."

Rich hoped that wasn't the case. Back in his office, he got Marcus Warren on the phone.

"The reason Bob can't ship the order is that your bag and sample suppliers are screw-ups. We have no samples of Woolens and the lingerie bags the supplier sent are cosmetic bags or something like that, according to Bob's description. If you get me the right stuff in here by tomorrow at noon, then the promo items will ship on time. I'm going to check with Miami to see if they can help us. So I'll need you to find out if the promotional stuff can go to Miami as well. By the way, whoever you've got dealing with vendors needs to cross this outfit off their list. Bob tells me he's been on the phone with the guy every day for two weeks."

"Well, Rich, next time tell Bob to call me."

"How about we figure out a way to avoid a next time?"

"I'm all ears," Marcus said.

"I don't know the answer. But this is a process redesign waiting to happen," Rich said.

It was after lunch when Marcus called back. He'd lined up a shipment of bags and samples to arrive in Charlotte before noon on Wednesday.

"But I have to know now if you want any of the giveaways to be sent to Miami," he told Rich.

"No such luck. Carlos can't help us out with this, but he is going to take care of a large Whitehead order we've got pending. At least that will clear out some of the orders that this Rollins thing is throwing behind.

"One more thing, Marcus, I think we're going to do a cross-functional team with the Whitehead account. If it goes well we'll try something similar with the Rollins account. Can you use your great charm and smooth things out with Rollins until we can get to their team?"

"Can you ship on-time?" Marcus asked.

"Like I said, if the bags and the samples arrive on-time, we'll have our shipment out of here by Friday," Rich said.

"Music to my ears. I'll see what I can do with Rollins," Marcus said.

Rich had barely put the phone down when the intercom buzzed.

"Melissa's on line two," Barbara said.

Rich picked up the phone. "Hi, hon. How's it going?"

"I'm so mad I could spit." Melissa didn't sound happy at all.

"Interested in playing professional baseball."

"Rich, please, this is serious," Melissa said.

"I'm a little aggravated myself, but you first. What's wrong?"

"The guys at Sewell & Prather are just trying to make my life hell. They are insisting that I take the stock instead of more money," Melissa said.

"Tell them no," Rich said.

"I tried that. They say they won't agree to it."

"I thought these guys were chomping at the bit. What do you think happened?" Rich asked.

"How am I supposed to know? I think they are worried that I'm not going to stay," Melissa answered.

"Maybe you should give it to them straight. Tell them you'll stay six months and no longer."

"I don't know. That might wreck the deal. I don't want to mess it up." Melissa sounded worried.

"Well, you have to decide what's most important. I can't do that for you."

"I don't expect you to do it for me, great swami. I just needed you to listen." Melissa's tone lightened a bit. "So how is your day going?"

"So far the good, the bad and before it's all over, I imagine, the ugly. We've got to revamp the entire DC to get an order out because someone else didn't deliver on-time. I don't know what time I'll be getting home," Rich said.

"Okay. Did you remember that Andrew has a home game tonight?" Melissa asked.

"It's on my calendar, but it doesn't look like I'll make it."

"What's the problem? Another starlet picketing your operation?" Melissa kidded.

"No. It's all about that one order. It's promotional merchandise for one of our bigger clients. We don't have the giveaway items to ship with the product, our *Slimmies*. So Bob's had a zillion *Slimmies* taking up space for three weeks and now he's going to have to use everybody here to get them out on time," Rich answered.

"So you can't let Bob handle it?"

"Ordinarily, I could. But I'm asking him to go way above the call of duty. This account is tricky right now. So I can't expect him to go it alone."

"Andrew will understand," Melissa said.

"I know, but I hate to miss his games when I'm in town. Maybe I can at least catch the end." Rich didn't sound too convinced. In fact, he didn't believe it himself.

"I'll save your supper. See you tonight."

Before Rich could tell her not to worry about the Sewell & Prather deal, she hung up. It concerned him that she seemed to have her heart set on it. As he went to look for Bob, Rich wondered what would happen if Melissa's deal fell through. If Sewell & Prather were this interested, maybe she could find another firm that wanted to buy AdWorks. No question, he had to find time for a decent discussion with Melissa.

Bob wasn't in his office, Darla thought he might be in the loading dock area. Rich donned a pair of safety glasses and found Bob on one of the docks.

"Miami can't help us with the *Slimmies.*" Rich shouted above the noise of a passing fork lift. "The best they can offer is to give us some relief on the Whitehead order. I told Carlos I'd get all the information from you and get back to him."

They walked back to Bob's office, and between the two of them, they reworked the warehouse priorities to accommodate the Rollins order. Several other orders, their status already hot, were also pushed back and Rich planned to check first thing Wednesday morning with his other DCs to see if they could offer any help on those.

The crowd was gone and the lights were out at the high school gym long before Rich left the office on Tuesday.

"*People start solving their problems before they figure out what they really are. You can't change what you don't see. The ones that are really scary are the ones that think they get it when they don't.*"

— *Wes Lucci to one of his fellow quality inspectors at Stabler over coffee and a honey bun before work, February*

CHAPTER TEN

"Let me see your license and registration please."

"Was I speeding?" Of all mornings to get pulled over, Rich couldn't believe it.

The police officer held out his hand, his face indicating a serious violation—murder, maybe or grand larceny, not speeding. Despite the early morning hour, the officer wore mirrored sun shades. He looked to be all of eighteen. Rich fumed, these guys get younger every day. It was hard to believe the guy was old enough to drive, let alone carry a gun.

"We'll get to that in a minute, sir. Let me see your license first."

Rich pulled his driver's license from his wallet and dug through the glove compartment for his white registration card. As he handed them out the window, he tried to smother the volcanic activity in his head and look friendly. He managed a smile.

"Look officer, I've got a flight in forty minutes. I'm in a real hurry."

"Sir, if you're dead on the road, the flight will leave without you anyway." The officer turned on his heel with all the precision of Schwarzenegger in a Terminator movie. Rich could have sworn he affected the movie star's accent when he said, "I'll be back."

"Couldn't we do this another time?" Rich shouted at the officer's retreating back. Geez, give a guy a leather jacket and a motorcycle and he thinks he rules the world.

Rich slapped the steering wheel. Forty minutes until his flight left for Boston and the airport was still a good twenty minutes from where the Suburban sat on the roadside, the blue lights of the motorcycle flashing a warning beacon behind it. How fast could he have been going anyway?

"Eighty-five, sir," the officer returned and informed Rich, using a tone that once again indicated a felonious act.

Rich signed the ticket without looking up again. With a small miracle, he could still make his flight.

"Take it easy on the speed and have a great day, sir." The officer's expression never changed. He could have easily said, "Try not to shoot anyone else."

Rich didn't particularly appreciate being called sir, either. It seemed like he had aged a year since Tuesday, but he didn't look that old, did he?

Wednesday had passed in a blur. The shipment of lingerie bags and detergent samples arrived before noon. Rich spent the day preparing for his meeting with Donald and Walter on Thursday and helped Bob transform the DC into an efficient shrink-wrap operation. Rich alternated between feeling exhilarated about all that was going on and despairing that they wouldn't meet Donald's challenge. Of course, he'd snapped at Kelly when he got home on Wednesday night, causing Melissa to raise her eyebrows at him. He felt he wasn't being any help to Melissa as far as the Sewell & Prather offer went. No wonder he was driving eighty-five. The airport loomed in front of him as he promised himself that he would do better.

He lucked into a close parking space and raced through security down the concourse to the gate, only to find the flight delayed by weather in Boston. Forty-five minutes later, he sank into his seat on the airplane and thought the rest of the day had to get better.

"Cream or sugar with that coffee?"

"Just black, thanks," Rich said.

The flight attendant handed him a sweet roll to go with his coffee. She reminded Rich of his high school sweetheart, Elaine. The last time he had seen Elaine, she looked about forty pounds heavier and a lot grayer than he remembered. If Melissa kept up with this stuff about a new baby, he'd be the only guy at the thirty-fifth reunion with a newborn. And when he got stopped for speeding the cop would tell him how cute his grandkid was.

"Ladies and gentlemen, this is Captain Haynes talking to you from the flight deck. The bad news is that the weather in Boston is rainy and overcast.

The good news is if you're staying around for the afternoon, the waterworks are supposed to clear up and it will be an unseasonably warm sixty degrees."

Rich sipped his coffee and looked over his notes one last time, thinking ahead to his presentation. What did he want Donald and Walter to do and how could he make them do it? He wanted them to buy into the plan of crossfunctional teaming for the Whitehead account. He wanted them to go ahead with the software installation and he wanted the funding to allow him to move forward with the change process. Larry and Denise were coming in to present information about their proposed system. Rich's goal was to have his part of the presentation done and the 'Dynamic Duo' sold on the concept in fifteen minutes. Fifteen minutes to convince Walter and Donald that what they were doing was important. Then Denise and Larry could present and then, well then, who knew?

Rich took a magazine out of his briefcase. He'd spotted an article on demand flow leadership and hadn't had a chance to read it yet.

• • • • • • • • • •

Why Demand Flow Leadership?

There are only three problems with the philosophy of Supply Chain Management. Unfortunately, the three problems are the words "supply," "chain" and "management."

The word supply is wrong as it indicates an obsolete "push" mentality. The philosophy behind push says, "If I build it, the orders will come." In today's highly competitive, streamlined, customized marketplace, this philosophy will result in high inventory levels, high operating costs and poor customer service. Therefore, the word "supply" is wrong, and instead, the word "demand" should be used. "Demand" indicates pull and reflects a philosophy that, "The customer tells me what they want and I will quickly provide it." Replacing the word "supply" with "demand" allows for reducing inventories and cost and enhancing service.

The word "chain" is wrong as it indicates individual, discrete links that are viewed as an entity unto themselves. The word "chain" should be replaced with the word "flow" (think pipeline) to indicate continuous movement. The "chain" thought process often results in link optimization as opposed to the "flow" thought process that takes a top-down, totally integrated approach to achieve the satisfaction of the ultimate customer.

The word "management" is wrong in that it implies a static environment of control and measurement. With today's SKU proliferation and customer performance, customer responsiveness and inventory reduction demands, what is needed is not static control and measurement, but the "leadership" to harness the energy of change, to pursue continuous improvement and achieve peak-to-peak performance.

Therefore, the philosophy with which our warehouses must function today is not Supply Chain Management but Demand Flow Leadership (DFL). True DFL can only be achieved via a continuously improving, customer-oriented approach of Demand Flow Leadership where we pull product through the pipeline, while harnessing the energy of change in pursuit of peak-to-peak performance.

The biggest challenge to organizations pursuing Demand Flow Leadership is the link of expertise that needs to be developed within organizations. To be successful in DFL, a Total Operations capability must be pursued. This Total Operations capability must consist of:

1. Logistics: To ensure the current distribution network and logistics methods.

2. Manufacturing: To ensure the proper products are efficiently and effectively produced at the right time and in the right quantity.

3. Warehousing: To ensure orders are efficiently and effectively filled and all customer requirements are fulfilled.

4. Organizational Excellence: To ensure a logistics, manufacturing and warehousing focus on the process of continuous improvement.

5. Maintenance: To ensure that operations are protected from breakdown and sufficient inventories will exist to cover reliability and maintainability problems.

6. Quality: To ensure the defective product is not produced as insufficient inventories will exist to cover for non-conforming production.

If one of these capabilities is not present, an organization will stumble in creating a DFL environment.

So, how should you proceed on your Demand Flow Leadership journey? The first step is to work with your leadership from awareness to understanding and acceptance of the philosophy shift from Supply Chain Management to Demand Flow Leadership. Second, you need to assess your Total Operations capability, determine where you fall short and then obtain the technical capability to address this shortfall. Third, you need to perform six assessments (Logistics, Manufacturing, Warehousing, Organizational Excellence, Maintenance, and Quality) on your "push" to "pull" transitions, *six assessments on your "chain" to "flow" transitions and six assessments on your "management" to "leadership" transitions.*

From these assessments will come a series of DFL measurements that can be used to track continuous improvement as well as prioritize opportunities for improvement. Pursuit of these opportunities will define the path forward to achieving enhanced performance. The continuation of this process of assessment, measurement, prioritizing opportunities and continuous improvement will result in achieving Demand Flow Leadership.

• • • • • • • • • •

The plane landed and the flight attendant who looked like Elaine announced, "Ladies and gentleman, the pilot has asked that you all remain seated as there is a slight problem with the door of the aircraft. Our ground crew is working to get this fixed as quickly as possible. We apologize for any inconvenience this may cause you."

Rich looked out his window. The sleeve that attached the aircraft to the terminal made several approaches toward the aircraft's door. Rich looked at his watch. He was already thirty minutes later than he'd told Donald's secretary after the first delay. He'd have to call her back when he got off the plane.

If he got off the plane.

Fifteen minutes later, the door dilemma solved, people crowded the aisle of the plane like lemmings rushing to the sea.

"Ick."

"Oh, gross."

"Watch your step."

As the door came into sight, Rich realized the source of the comments. The sleeve connecting to the plane had malfunctioned and there was a large gap through which rain poured on the departing passengers, a gauntlet of freezing water. A ground crew member tried to hold an umbrella over the departing passengers, but the rain blew beneath it. The way the umbrella bobbed and swayed, the guy would be lucky not to put someone's eye out. A perfect way to end the morning, Rich thought, as he dodged the umbrella and headed for the car rental area. If the Wright Brothers could only see what their invention had come to.

The day had to get better. This couldn't be an indication of how the meeting with Donald and Walter would go, could it?

"Personally, I don't see the difference if they call us all associates or they call us all employees. Doesn't seem like much of a change to me. How people treat you—that's what counts."

— Katrina Ballard discussing a new Stabler policy with her husband over supper at the K & W, February

CHAPTER ELEVEN

The conference room was empty when Rich arrived. The abstract paintings that covered the conference room walls reminded him of pictures that Melissa and Andrew had done when they were in grade school. If they'd only saved them, they could be independently wealthy by now. Rich organized his presentation package. He'd checked in with Donald's secretary on his way through. She let him know that Donald would be in shortly; he was tied up with a phone conversation.

Walter wandered in with the air of a lost child at the supermarket. "Mrs. Stabler, please retrieve your child from the service desk." That worked. Rich wished Walter's mother would retrieve him. What was it Kelly used to say to Andrew when he annoyed her? "Poof and be gone." That would work, too. Rich decided that his stress level must be off the meter if all it took to set him off was Walter walking into the room.

"Rich, what have you been able to find out about those budget overages in packing?" The whine in Walter's voice crawled over Rich like fingernails scraping down a chalkboard.

"Remember, Walter, it has to do with packaging. We're doing so much custom packaging in Charlotte, we've eaten our packing budget and our packaging budget, too."

Rich heard Donald's voice in the hallway right before he appeared in the doorway.

"Good morning. You ready to ride, Rich? We've got a lot of territory to cover."

Donald Stabler strode across the room toward Rich's end of the conference table. Every time Rich thought he was accustomed to Donald's eccentric ways, Donald surprised him. 'The Donald's' latest outfit resembled a corporate Hell's Angel. He was dressed in a black leather jacket that sported a Harley insignia and matching pants with a T-shirt that completed the outfit.

"I keep one of my bikes in the parking garage." Donald gestured in the general direction of the parking area. "I'm going to ride this afternoon with some old friends. Makes me feel young. Get some of my best ideas out riding," he explained.

Rich hoped Donald didn't get any more ideas for mergers and acquisitions. Maybe that's what he should do, get himself a Harley. Melissa could ride in the back and they could just hook a side car on for the new baby.

"What you're going to get, Donald, is a good case of pneumonia." Walter chided his father.

Then Walter could run Stabler. That was a pleasant thought. Rich's sweet roll from his earlier flight did a flip in his stomach.

Larry and Denise arrived, each carrying a steaming cup of coffee and a sheaf of overhead transparencies. Rich launched right into his plan.

"Basically, Donald, we have identified a need for a crossfunctional team. This team, the Whitehead Service Team, will be responsible for working with Whitehead in every area that we deal with them: the distribution center, sales and marketing, planning , manufacturing, customer service, and finance and information technology. As you can see from the list, the team members we have chosen are all well versed in their areas. As a crossfunctional team they will be altering, actually transforming, the Stabler culture. Not only will we meet Whitehead's needs, we will be aware of them before Whitehead. Then we can change in order to accommodate the needs they have and those we anticipate they are going to have."

"Because you're not as familiar with our teaming process, I've listed the types of teams for you. If you look down the list you'll see that this group is really a crossfunctional design team. We're expecting them to do blue-sky, clean-sheet, greenfield innovation."

"That reminds me of an old Navy term we had, CAVU. Ceiling and visibility unlimited." True to form, Donald couldn't resist a military reference. However, since he was wearing a Harley outfit that day, he peppered the conversation with biking and racing metaphors as well, bouncing back and forth between racing and military references.

Walter ignored his father and huffed at Rich, "I thought that they were going to improve performance."

"You're thinking of a functional work team. Again, if you look at the chart, you see that functional work teams work down in the organization to improve performance. They breathe life into the process of continuous improvement and unleash our best asset, people. The Whitehead Service Team is supposed to be much broader in scope. These people are our change agents; they should be thinking out-of-the-box. That process will then lead to more functional and crossfunctional work teams."

"You're quite the expert, aren't you, Rich?" Walter commented.

"Actually, Valerie Wagner in human resources is our real expert. She's really facilitated the teaming process in Charlotte."

"Well, how are you going to get everybody driving on the same track?" Donald wanted to know.

Back to racing, Rich thought. "Our Leadership Team and our Communication Team are both working hard to make sure everyone knows we're about to take off in a new direction. The Communication Team has designed several things to help with that process. I'd like for you and Walter to come down to Charlotte when they get the first two pieces of the puzzle worked out. We're trying to get people excited about change, we're trying to emphasize Stabler's commitment to change, and we're trying to help people see that we're not Big Daddy looking out for them. Get them to take charge of their own career paths at Stabler. Of course, culturally we've got to be the kind of company that lets them do that."

Walter spoke up. "Rich, one thing that really concerns me is this training issue. Lisa tells me that your woman in human resources is telling her that training is not a priority. Since when is training not a priority in the Stabler organization?" At one end of the table, Rachel and Bob chatted.

"Training is important, Walter. What Valerie is saying is that training for the sake of training is useless, a waste of time and money. If we're seeing teaming as a process, not just another program, then the most effective way to train is just-in-time."

"Just-in-time training?"

"That's right. Remember, it's uncover, discover and recover."

"Sure," Walter said, looking not at all sure.

"Uncover is when the team finds a need for training. This need is identified by the team, for the team. Discover follows when the team actually receives the training and then recover is the third part of the process where the team puts that training to work. The team has the information that it needs, when it needs it, and two thousand others in the organization that don't need it are not wasting their time sitting through unnecessary training."

"That makes sense to me," Donald said. "Walter, have Lisa get with Valerie about the specifics. Now, Rich, explain all the people on this list. Why are you the team sponsor?"

"Back a week ago when you gave me the assignment of a complete overhaul, I looked to see where we could make the most impact in the shortest period of time. Whitehead was the obvious choice. So since I saw the need for the team, I became its sponsor. In this case I also wrote the charter, but a sponsor doesn't always have to write the team charter."

"But I want you to oversee this," Donald said.

"Oh, I will," Rich replied. "Sometimes team sponsors are only that. They see a need and speak up. Sometimes to make their case they also go out and collect statistics and other information to help define the potential for improvement. Other times, team sponsors go on to become the team leader or team liaison or simply a team member. In this case, I will be the team leader and Valerie Wagner from human resources and a member of the Leadership Team will serve as our team liaison. If we can get a go-ahead from you here today, I can schedule a meeting for the first of next week."

The rest of the meeting went well. The group asked a few more questions about the teaming chart before Larry and Denise spoke. They provided a presentation that was short and to the point on the new computer system and software package.

"Splendid," Donald slapped the table. "Information technology is our pit crew. They're going to get this car back on the track and into the race. And you're going to do it as fast as possible. Right Larry and Denise?"

You had to give Donald credit, he was always thinking. On the other hand, Walter could never come up with anything original to say. His favorite phrases included, "Don't count your chickens before they're hatched," and "A bird in the hand is worth two in the bush."

During a break, Denise leaned over to Rich and whispered, "If Walter says, 'It's not the size of the dog in the fight, it's the size of the fight in the dog,' one more time, I'm going to have to growl and bite him."

Rich nodded. "Better watch it, he could be rabid."

As the time for open discussion wound down, Rich turned to Donald.

"Donald, one more thing I wanted to talk to you about. Larry mentioned something the other day about a reorganization of DCs."

"What reorganization?" Donald looked at Larry and Walter.

"Walter has been talking about cutting—"

Walter interrupted Larry. "We've been talking about closing some of these new DCs as a cost-cutting measure." Walter tried to look tough, but succeeded only in looking like he was feeling the full effects of a Polish sausage from Fenway Park.

Rich chose his words carefully, "I can understand the concern to cut costs, but I think we best have a good idea of what we're doing now and where we're going in the future before we start closing down operations. One day we may wish we'd left them open. We're benchmarking and getting our own baseline data now. Then we can look realistically at which locations are the best, or if we need to do new locations entirely."

Donald held up a hand to silence Walter's reply. "I think we can all agree that no one knows what we actually need. No one closes anything until you get a handle on this."

A temporary reprieve, Rich thought. Reprieve from what still remained to be seen.

"Fine by me. We're going to have our hands full getting this new system on-line. In fact, if no one else has any questions, we're going to move along," Larry said.

Larry and Denise stood.

"Rich, I'll call you once I talk to the software people and get a firm date," Denise said.

After Larry and Denise left, Rich packed his notes into his briefcase. If he could get an earlier flight, he might get some work done this afternoon in Charlotte. He had his coat half on when Donald's secretary rang in. "Rich, Bob Ketchum is on line one for you. Says it's urgent."

Rich felt his stomach tighten. What could have possibly gone wrong with the Rollins order?

Bob sounded out of breath. "Rich, the girdles are missing."

"What?" Rich noticed Donald and Walter staring. He turned slightly as if that could somehow cut them off from the conversation.

"We're missing a couple thousand girdles. The damn things have been in our way for three weeks now. And when we need em, vamoose, they're gone. I bet we're three thousand short on this order. I swear, when I find out who is behind this, their ass is out of here."

Rich focused on the abstract painting in front of him, aware that Donald and Walter were still staring. The bright blue orbs of the painting wound together. Red splashed across the top of them. It looked like a technique that Kelly had used to paint the wall in her room when she was four. The red made Rich think of blood, his own blood. The bright orbs began to take the shape of Walter's head. Rich closed his eyes to focus his thoughts.

"That's not the big issue at the moment. Our priority is to get the order shipped. We'll have to figure out the other stuff later." It was entirely possible with the way things were going at the DCs that no one stole the *Slimmies*, Rich thought. They might simply be lost. "Where are we going to get three thousand gird—*Slimmies*, in time to get them out tomorrow?"

"The only thing I know to do is call the other DCs to see if they can get them to us today," Bob answered. "I've checked with the plants—nobody has any. Three thousand won't take that long to wrap, but you can't wrap them if you don't have them."

"I'll call Mike Graves in Chicago and Greg Anderson here in Boston. Make sure your guys have checked every possible location. Get the rest of the product that you have taken care of and I'll get back to you."

"Will do," Bob said.

The phone clicked in Rich's ear. He placed the receiver down gently as if it were a stem of crystal and turned to face Walter and Donald. "A glitch in the Rollins order. We're short on some product. Nothing major."

Walter looked concerned. "Rich, are you sure? I mean how can you have a shortage? Don't you have people counting those things?"

"Yes, Walter. I can't tell you what went wrong until I get there. Bob is investigating. All I know is we've got to fix it."

Donald frowned. "Rich, they've started the race and it sounds like the others are leaving us in the dust. You best get the pedal to the metal."

"That's right, Rich. I've been telling you—"

Donald interrupted. "Walter, the man says he is fixing it. He knows there's a problem. Blaming is useless at this point. Besides, don't you have some work to do on the Mitko acquisition?"

Rich tried to block the word acquisition out of his mind as he began calling the DCs to locate additional *Slimmies*. There were enough *Slimmies* at the Boston DC to finish out the Rollins order. Greg Anderson, the DC manager, reminded Rich that "Charlotte owed him one now."

"I'll let Bob know that."

Donald's secretary buzzed in again. "Rich, Kurt Thomas with corporate communications is on line one for you."

Kurt sounded perturbed. "Rich, this Rita Sue woman is all over the place again and she wants to talk to you. Swears she's going to call a press conference unless she does."

"Kurt, what does she think I'm going to do for her? She's got you. Your job's communications. Communicate."

Once again, Walter and Donald turned their attention to Rich.

Kurt laughed. "I could communicate if the woman were interested in what I have to say. From what I gather, she thinks you have the most honest-looking face in the company. As for me, I must look like a second-generation, used-car salesman."

"For crying out loud, Kurt. I'm in Boston today, flying back to Charlotte this evening. I was just trying to get an earlier flight. I've got a full schedule and I don't have time to hold a starlet's hand. This woman needs help." This was Kurt's problem and somehow he'd managed to throw it over to Rich.

"Hey Rich, I'm just telling you what the woman wants. She's shooting a movie up on the Cape. Maybe you could work out a face-to-face later today. Here's her number." Kurt read Rich a phone number. "Let me know if you want me there."

When Rich hung up, Donald asked. "Another problem?"

"It's Rita Sue Fox. She's still unhappy and wants to talk to me. Says she's going to call a press conference if she doesn't hear from me."

"Communist pink-o," Donald pronounced.

"Well, it would be nice if she'd decide to pick on some shoe manufacturer. Anyway, she's shooting a film up on the Cape, so she's close by. Kurt thinks we should try for a meeting since I'm here anyway."

Donald swaggered a bit in his leather jacket. "Tell her to come on by and I'll explain life to her. All this emotional agony and crying and gnashing of teeth hasn't kept her from cashing our checks. Before this is over, I'm going to find out which of those dimwits in the media group thought this damn campaign was a good idea."

Walter volunteered nothing. As Rich recalled, Walter had been heavily in favor of an advertising campaign with a celebrity spokesperson. Walter offered Rich no suggestions. His favorite trick was to wait and point out the flaws in whatever Rich did.

Rich had to get through Bev, the efficient assistant, to speak with Rita Sue.

"Miss Fox, Rich Morrison."

"Oh Rick, call me Rita Sue. It's lovely of you to phone." Rita Sue gushed like she hadn't just threatened Kurt Thomas to bring the call about. "I mean, Mr. Thomas is a lovely man, but I feel like I'm getting the corporate run-around. I said to myself, if I could only talk to Rick he could do something about this whole thing."

"Actually, it's Rich and I tell you Miss Fox, Rita Sue. I'm in Boston today and have to catch a flight back to Charlotte at two this afternoon. Maybe we could talk over the phone."

"Kurt told me you might be in Boston. We've got an open day on the schedule so you just sit tight. I can get Bev to rebook you on a later flight and then I'll be down there—," Rita Sue's voice muffled as she turned the phone aside.

"Bev, how long before we can be in Boston?"

Her voice came back strong. "Bev says we should be there by two. If she rebooks your flight, that'll give us a few minutes to chat before you have to leave for the airport. Now, I'm going to put Bev on the line and I want you to give her your airline information and directions to where you are. I'm not at all good with that sort of thing."

Rich gave Bev directions to Stabler headquarters and assured her he would handle his own plane reservations. "If I can't rebook on the six o'clock flight, I'll let you know."

"Well, I hope it's no problem because Rita Sue goes postal when she doesn't get what she wants."

Rich assumed going postal would negatively impact Stabler's relationship with Rita Sue.

"Is that woman coming here?" Donald wanted to know as soon as Rich put down the phone.

"I believe so. I really don't know what I can tell her. I don't know what she's been told about our overseas contractors. I guess I'll get Kurt Thomas to debrief me."

"Well, I'll be here with you. It's time someone explained reality to this little socialist ninny."

Great, Rich thought, shootout at the 'O.K. Corral.' Donald should have worn his spurs and his ten-gallon hat today. And who would be right in the middle as the dust cleared? Rich Morrison, man of action. The guy in the middle of a gunfight usually got shot full of holes.

He noticed a spot on his tie and excused himself to go try and clean it off. You never knew when you were leaving home in the morning if you might have to 'take a meeting' with a Hollywood type. It really wasn't 'take a meeting' in this case, it was have one shoved down your throat. The speeding ticket was starting to look like the highlight of his day. He hadn't realized at the time that this was a motorcycle theme day.

● ● ● ● ● ● ● ● ●

When the plane touched down in Charlotte that evening, Rich resisted the temptation to kneel down and kiss the ground. Instead, he drove to the DC where he found Bob Ketchum supervising operations that looked like December 23rd at the North Pole. The stares he got from a couple of the line supervisors were as frigid as the North Pole winds.

Bob bounced from one spot to the other, patting backs and helping speed the flow of work. He came over when one of the guys pointed Rich out to him.

"You look like the Energizer Bunny," Rich said.

"More like Ricochet Rabbit. These are the last ones. Everything ships tomorrow and if I never see another girdle in my life, I'll be happy."

"Did you ever locate the missing ones?"

"No. But Rhonda over in order entry is looking a little slimmer." Bob laughed at his own joke. "Seriously, if they're in this warehouse, we can't find them."

"You're sure we received them?"

"Positive. We've got the bill of lading on the shipment and the confirmation. Barbara said you had to change your flight. Had more problems at headquarters?"

"Problems with a capital P. Actually, a capital R."

"What?"

"No, who. Our old friend, Rita Sue. She insisted on speaking to me. Donald insisted on speaking to her. It was Fourth of July from the minute she got there. He didn't call her a socialist ninny to her face, but it was close. My goal was to keep them in their corners until the bell rang and to keep anybody from hitting below the belt. Other than that, I was just trying to dodge punches myself. I thought we were going to have to do CPR on Kurt Thomas." Rich laughed ruefully. "That's what he gets for trying to pass her off to me."

"So what happened?"

"Well, no one got a KO. More like a Mexican standoff. Rita Sue and Kurt and Donald agreed to meet again. I promised to check back in a few weeks to see how she's doing. Like what I have time to do is hold this woman's hand."

"I wouldn't mind that."

"Meeting with Rita Sue Fox is like getting run over by a freight train."

"So what did Donald think?"

"You know Donald. Freight train meets the 'Man of Steel.' I think he enjoyed every minute of it. Today, he had on—get this—a motorcycle jacket and leather pants."

Bob hitched up his already bulging belt. "I've been thinking about getting me a pair of leather pants. I didn't know they were in the dress code."

"On you, they're definitely not," Rich said as he headed for his office to call it a night.

Rich dreamed of *Slimmies* that night. He was at a party, everyone there wore *Slimmies* on their heads, even Rita Sue Fox.

Friday morning, he didn't even make it in the office door before he heard Bob Ketchum's voice. Bob paced up and down in front of Barbara's desk, his voice just decibels below an all-out shout. Barbara looked concerned and nodded her head from time to time. She obviously realized the futility of trying to slow Bob down.

When he saw Rich, he quit pacing. "Team work. You want to know team work? George Nader says that every one of those damn girdle boxes has got to be opened. Every one. Tell me I didn't have my guys here all night so that quality could screw up the schedule. George knew we were under the gun. If his guys needed to open the damn boxes they should have been here all night like the rest of us."

"Okay, Bob. I'll handle it. You look like you're running ragged. Maybe you should take the afternoon off," Rich said.

"Did you forget that ship list? I've got orders to get out that should have gone days ago," Bob answered.

"Well, do me a favor. Go take a few minutes to calm down. You're not going to get any orders out from the Cardiac Unit at Charlotte Memorial."

Rich found George Nader in discussion with one of his supervisors. Rich could never think of her name. Sarah, no. Sandra, no. Samantha, that was it.

Samantha excused herself after she and Rich exchanged "hellohowareyous."

"I know why you're here, Rich, and just let me say, I've got my people working as hard as they can go on this Rollins order," George said.

"George, we can't delay the shipment. There's got to be something that we can do to get it out of here," Rich commented.

"I don't know what it would be, Rich, unless you want to put some of the other personnel on it."

"Let me ask you this, George. Exactly how many defective pieces have you found?"

George looked away.

Rich waited.

"None."

"None. For crying out loud, George, how much of the order have you finished?"

George shifted his feet before answering. "About fifty percent."

"Fifty percent with no defects and you're going to hold the damn order up because you want to look through every box." Rich rubbed his neck. "George, it can't happen. You are going through every box, aren't you?"

"Yes. Rich, I take my responsibility to deliver a quality product very seriously." George looked at Rich as if he'd asked him to sell state secrets to Saddam Hussein.

"And the key word is deliver. We've got to deliver. Not one error and you're opening every box—that does not get the order out the door." Rich chopped one hand against the other palm. "Now, you figure how many more boxes you want to open, but whatever happens, that order is leaving this warehouse today."

Rich didn't try to keep the anger and disappointment out of his voice. George's refusal to budge on quality issues seemed to be mushrooming now that they had started talking about changing the process. The ship was leaving the dock and George had one foot on the dock and one foot on the boat trying to keep it in the same place. Rich needed for George to see that that was a losing strategy.

Bob came walking up the aisle. "I've got thirty extra pickers that can help you finish, George. They're over in Ramen Fatehi's department, extension 157. He's expecting your call."

George nodded his head in acknowledgment and sighed long and low. You would have thought he was Joan of Arc right before they lit the kindling.

"Good work," Rich told Bob as they left the quality area and walked back towards his office.

At noon, when the Leadership Team assembled, George reported that the order would be shipped on-time. The meeting began with Rachel being assigned recorder and Irving reviewing the Model of Success. Rich discussed the last meeting and the group went through a quick run-down of their previous action items.

At the request of Rachel and Bob, Jay Bhutto, a senior analyst from the Warehouse Information Systems department, reported on the results of their current shipping profile and performance review.

Rachel and Bob reported their dates for the benchmarking trips. Bob couldn't resist adding, "That is, if we don't have to ship a gazillion girdles again."

Valerie laughed. "Bob, they're *Slimmies*, not girdles. Girdles are out, *Slimmies* are in."

"Could somebody explain to me the difference?"

"The language is all wrong. The concept. When you think of a girdle you think restrictive, pinching body armor. The words, *Slimmies*, makes you think of garments that shape you, allowing that new dress to fit easily. Something that works with you to create a fashion statement." Rachel's voice rose and fell in melodic tones as she described the *Slimmies'* best features.

"Damn, Rachel, that was good. If that's not in our catalog, it ought to be. I'm thinking about becoming a cross dresser just listening to you talk about it," Irving said.

Irving answered their earlier questions about the WMS and then he added, "But I've talked with Denise and Larry and it seems to me that we need to include a DRP package as well."

"DRP being?" Rachel asked.

"DRP being Distribution Requirements Planning system that will look globally at all points in our supply chain," Irving said.

"That's pipeline to you," Rich said, "Supply chain is out, pipeline is in. It's that whole girdle, *Slimmies* thing. One is restrictive, the other is flowing."

Everyone laughed.

"Rachel, what has the Communication Team come up with?"

"We've got a commercial for change that will knock your socks off. We'd like for it to premier in two weeks at the Leadership Team meeting. If everyone likes it, then we'll take it on the road," Rich said.

"I should have my first take at the Personal Path Forward kit by then as well," Valerie added.

"The Whitehead Service Team is meeting for the first time on Monday," Rich said.

"That was fast," Irving said.

"The statement, 'Donald wants this,' tends to light a fire under people," Rich explained. "So we should have our next Leadership Team meeting at the regular time on Tuesday. I need a minute with you, George, if we're all done?"

Everyone rose, nodding agreement as they left.

"So what's your take on the Rollins order?" Rich asked George.

"Like I told you at the beginning of the meeting, it's going out just like everyone wants. The real test is what happens when the customers start opening those boxes."

"I think you're right, George. So what I'm going to ask Rachel's customer service people to do is to follow up by phone with each of the Rollins' orders. That'll give us immediate feedback on the quality."

"That sounds good to me." George almost smiled.

Rich couldn't decide if the smile was because George was pleased they were going to follow up so closely or if he was pleased because he thought they would find a significant number of errors in the unchecked cartons.

"Valerie is going to help you rework the charter for the Quality Team. I think our focus may need to be on getting your people to work with our suppliers. Our biggest quality issues seem to be order fulfillment and meeting ship schedules, not the quality of our products."

Later that afternoon the new Quality Team charter came across Rich's desk for his review.

There was also a reminder fax from Melissa's administrative assistant that Andrew's basketball team had an away game that night. Across the bottom Melissa's assistant had scribbled a note: "Barbara, please make sure he sees this."

Rich stopped by Bob's office in the late afternoon. "How's everything looking down here?"

"Great. Ramen said some of his people complained about being switched over to quality today. That's something we need to work on, Rich. People need to get over that it's not-my-job mentality."

Rich couldn't even begin to fathom the irony of Bob's observation. The original not-my-job man seeing that you do what needs to be done.

As if Bob could read his mind, he leaned back and said, "I know I've learned that we've got to own the whole thing from start to finish."

Maybe this thing could fly after all.

Bob continued, "Now all we've got to do is figure out what happened to those three thousand girdles. Beg your pardon, those three thousand *Slimmies*."

They'd lost three thousand *Slimmies*, but maybe, just maybe, as Donald would say, they were winning the war.

"What was it Rich Morrison said about fear?"

"'We have nothing to fear, but fear itself.' I can't remember exactly who it was he said, said it first, believe it was some guy on the Winston Cup circuit."

"Must've been Dale Earnhardt. He's a tough one."

— Conversation on the packaging line at Stabler between Luke Sullivan and Billy Boyton after a Communication Forum, February

CHAPTER TWELVE

When Rich left the office that evening, the Suburban's interior felt like an old robe—comforting and warm. 'The Jack Thompson Show' had just begun.

"This evening my guest is Randall Heisling, vice president of LogisticsWorks, one of the leading third-party providers in the world. For the benefit of our viewers, tell us, Randall, exactly what a third-party provider does."

"Whatever the customer wants that's not immoral or illegal. LogisticsWorks handles all, or part, of the supply chain functions for our customers. We are capable of dealing with all the issues of distributing a customer's product, and in some cases, we even handle the flow of their raw materials as well. Some customers simply contract with us for space in a public warehouse, some customers have us handle a specific geographic area, and others, as I said earlier, have us doing soup to nuts."

Randall's voice was deep and full, reminding Rich of a mall Santa Claus.

"That sounds pretty extensive, but we all know third-party logistics is a fast growing area. What do you see as the greatest growth area for third-party providers?" Jack asked.

"As a third-party provider, we've seen our business take on all sorts of new dimensions. Over the last five years, value-added services have become very important to our customers. These services would include things like packaging, labeling, order picking and order fulfillment. The list of services that we offer is twenty-seven items long and growing. Warehousing involves dealing with customer satisfaction, knowing what the customer wants before he does, keeping up-to-date with the latest technology in Electronic Data Interchange, or EDI if you're into acronyms," Randall paused. "American companies spent $670 billion on distribution last year, so there is great concern that you spend your money wisely."

"$670 billion? That's amazing. But haven't companies been doing distribution all along? What's the big deal?"

"The pace of change is unbelievable, Jack. Today's customers want quality products, quality service and increasing value. Corporations know that. So if a company has decided to expand globally and has no global experience, they may turn to a third-party provider or a company may have far-reaching service areas that are more efficiently served by a third-party provider. Another reason companies turn to us is the high number of mergers and acquisitions, which cause a reevaluation of how the company does business. Or in some cases, a corporation may simply wish to reduce debt by selling off the buildings and machinery that are required to do distribution of any kind. Not to mention what it takes to run a world-class logistics operation."

"How do corporations know if a third-party is right for them?"

"The first thing that a company needs to look at is their baseline operation. What does it cost them to be in the distribution business? Then they have to ask themselves, is there any way they can alter that cost?"

"What sorts of questions should they be asking?" Jack asked.

"Things like, what is our percentage of on-time deliveries? What is the fastest we can turn around a customer's order? How much inventory do we carry as a safety net for flaws in our logistical system? The cost of carrying inventory is one of the largest in an inefficient operation." Randall added, "And, finally, where are you going as a company? Do you want to make logistics a core competency at your firm? If so, is it possible for you as a company to develop a meaningful competitive advantage in this non-core area?"

"Boy, those aren't easy questions," Jack said.

"No, certainly not. But a good third-party relationship should be a win/win non-adversarial relationship. So if you don't make the right choice about outsourcing to start with, both you and I are going to suffer," Randall said. "A simplified example of this. Several years ago, my daughter attended a women's college. I happened to talk with the Dean of Students at a Parents' Weekend function. She told me that the college's dietitian had retired a few years earlier.

Being progressive, the institution decided to outsource their food service. They took bids and selected a provider."

Randall continued, "After only one semester, the food service company came back and said, 'We're getting eaten alive.' Pardon my pun. 'We can't come close to meeting the needs of your students at our current contract price. We'd like out.'

"It seems that they placed a bid without ever studying the students at the college. Based on their vast experience elsewhere, they knew that a very small percentage of college students ate breakfast. Not my daughter and her classmates. Not only did they eat breakfast, they came back for seconds and thirds. They studied in the dining hall. They loaded up on breakfast breads to take to class. The college realized that they had a unique situation, agreed to allow the food service company out of their contract, hired a new dietitian and went back in the food service business.

"But the moral of this story is that nobody did their homework and it cost them. Chances are, had they asked the employees in the dining hall a few questions, they would have realized early on what they were up against. Which brings me to my next point.

"Develop a clear scope of work for third-party providers to bid on. If you are trying to establish a scope of work for a third-party provider, for heaven's sake, talk to the guys doing the job now."

"That makes sense," Jack said.

"Actually, Jack, it is easier said than done. These are the same people who are going to resist your outsourcing most heavily. This is going to change their livelihood. This is where your human resource area—as well as good leadership—is essential."

"Give us some examples of what is included in a scope of work."

"It should have basics like hours and days of operation, as well as the agreed fee structure, spelled out. The schedule of services and activities and anything that will specifically impact those activities. Operational considerations should include all pertinent activities such as product rotation, safety, quality and things of that nature. Any special services that don't fall under the normal schedule should be clearly outlined in the scope of work. All reporting requirements should be outlined completely. A properly developed scope of work makes your distribution concerns clear, both to yourself and to interested third-party providers."

"Okay," Jack said. "So we have our scope of work. How do we chose a provider that's a match for our needs?"

"That's a very involved process as well. Each provider should be evaluated on the basis of capability, philosophy, financial data, cost and service, and other things like their systems and details. Those who make the short list should then be given a request for proposal."

"Let me guess, the RFP should fully outline what you're looking for?"

"You're catching on, Jack. Scope of work, final customer requirements, information technology requirements, value-added services, location, specialized facility and equipment needs and management reporting requirements." Randall paused. "Then you get serious."

"Gee, I thought we already were," Jack said.

"Talk to their customers. Look at their use of information technology and other control systems. Are they flexible? Can they change with your needs? What about the location and the condition of their building and facilities? Is their geographic area of operation strategically advantageous? How deep are their pockets and their personnel? Make sure you've got total costs bid and finally, do they practice and appreciate continuous improvement from bottom to top in their company?"

"Wow, that's a mouthful," Jack said.

"And it needs to be. If you don't know these things going into a third-party relationship, you might as well try to build a house on quicksand."

"You mentioned total costs bid. I'm sure this varies a good bit with each of your contracts," Jack said. "But can you just speak to the issue of how you structure fees?"

"Again, because you're in a long-term relationship, fee structures tend to change, evolving over the course of the relationship. Basically, we see three structures used in determining fees. There is a unit rate, which, just as it implies, is an agreed-to charge on each unit handled. With a management fee structure, your company takes care of all the costs as they are billed and then you set a management fee to cover the logistics provider's overhead and profit. The other frequently seen option is the cost-plus structure. Just as it implies, you may pay the provider cost plus a percentage fee. Some companies add incentives for cost reduction and service enhancement. Very often, fee structures are variations and combinations of these three types: unit rate, management fee and cost-plus structuring."

"It seems that there has to be a high level of customization in all of this."

"Absolutely. There is no formula that's right for every situation," Randall agreed.

"What can you expect as your challenges if you choose a third-party provider?" Jack asked.

"Well, there is a lot more information out there, but still you're dealing with a tremendous amount of uncharted territory in third-party relationships. So you have to realize that there isn't a lot to go on and that you're pioneering the effort. Some days you're Christopher Columbus and some days you're Ralph Jeeter." Randall laughed.

"Who is Ralph Jeeter?"

"Ralph Jeeter predicted the end of the world. Seven different times. See, he was a pioneer, but not one that will be remembered.

"Your big challenge is your people challenge. Working with all employees to overcome their negative feelings. Particularly middle managers and front line people since they tend to be the most skeptical."

"People can make or break you," Jack commented.

"That's right," Randall said. "Look at how you reward people. If antiquated reward systems are in place and your overall savings don't show up on a particular manager's balance sheet, then chances are they're going to put up quite a fight. And who can blame them if you don't present a better reward scenario?"

"What other issues?" Jack asked.

"Consider that customer service changes could be harder to implement because they are no longer under your control," Randall said.

"What is your biggest challenge?" Jack asked.

"Those companies that talk quality, quality, quality and then buy price. As a provider, we're in it for the long haul. We want to establish long-term relationships. But long-term relationships require more communication and more time. They also yield much greater benefits. If you're not willing to commit that time up front to get systems operating and to work out the massive number of issues involved in third-party relationships, then chances of a divorce are strong."

"Sort of like the guy who says, 'Honey, I love you for who you are, but gain five pounds and I'm out of here.'"

"Exactly," Randall replied.

"What are some other things companies do that set them up for failure?" Jack asked.

"Sometimes these guys get so caught up in measuring numbers that they fail to see what the important numbers are. For instance, there was a 1942 football game between the Washington Redskins and the New York Giants. The Redskins really pounded the Giants; they ran and passed much farther than New York.

"So what was the problem, you ask. The problem was the score. The Giants won 14-7 because of a seventy-yard interception and a fifty-yard touchdown pass. When it came to first downs, the Redskins had fourteen and the Giants had zero, but that didn't matter because first downs aren't points. There are people out there measuring first downs instead of points."

"Sort of like those pictures that you can look at one way and see one thing and look at another way and see something completely different," Jack said.

"That's right. So you need to make sure you're focusing on the right picture," Randall agreed.

"Let's say that I'm a company sitting on the edge trying to decide about using a third-party provider. What is so significant about what you do for your clients?" Jack asked.

"Imagine a world in which you have the advantage of gaining expertise in systems, logistics and marketing without having to invest in human resources. LogisticsWorks and other world-class third-party logistics firms invest heavily to keep ourselves on the cutting edge of the logistics business. By keeping ourselves on the cutting edge, we keep your company there as well."

"What do you see as the biggest issue in success of third-party?"

"Communication. It is the core of every relationship. The place it succeeds or fails. Communicate across company lines, across functional lines and most importantly, between individuals. One-on-one communication is the heart and soul of success," Randall said.

"If you get into a situation that is not win/win and everyone agrees it is not salvageable, is there a way out?"

"Of course. Most contracts contain a notice clause that either party can exercise. The standard notice is somewhere between thirty and ninety days."

"So you aren't signing your life away?" Jack asked

"No. Not by any means. But again, I want to emphasize the importance of allowing your provider enough time to complete the massive amount of changes that have to be made. Both you and your third-party partner should be looking together to the future. Seeing the possibilities and making the best of opportunities," Randall said.

Rich pulled into the parking lot of the high school just as Jack announced that the lines were open for callers. As he walked toward the gym, Rich wondered if he would find Thomas Sewell perched, like some advertising vulture, on the bleacher next to Melissa again. But Melissa sat alone, beckoning him up as soon as she saw him. Both teams were still out on the floor for their opening warm-ups.

"So how are you?" Melissa smiled and reached up to pick off a piece of fuzz that clung to Rich's suit.

"I consider it a real coup that I'm not actively bleeding. How was your day?" Rich asked.

"Not bad." Melissa flicked the fuzz from her finger into the air. "But I'm certainly not sorry that I have two days to look forward to without having to take one phone call from a client. I'm definitely ready for a little recharge. You know what happened with the Harrell account, I'd give the business to Sewell & Prather right now."

The way she'd said it, so off-handed, Rich knew he was supposed to know about the Harrell account. What was it? She'd fired the account manager? They'd pulled the account? The Harrell account was really a front for the Mafia to launder money? Rich hated when he couldn't remember.

Melissa helped him out. "You remember the Harrell account. He's pulled the ads and threatened to sue. Word is, business is on the rocks and this is his way of getting out of the bill."

"Tell him to tee it up then. No way you should let him walk," Rich said.

"I'm not planning to, but I'd sure rather spend my energy on something else other than lawsuits."

A whistle on the floor signaled the opening jump. An injury to the starting forward put Andrew on the floor. The second play of the game, the guard came across the half-court line and threw Andrew a high pass. He jumped to get it and the player guarding him pushed him as he came down. The ref blew the whistle and rolled his arms.

Rich came up off the bleacher. "Travel?" He threw his hands in the air and yelled, "Are you blind? It was a body slam."

Melissa pulled on his sleeve. "Not so loud."

The next play for the Wildcats, Andrew threw a great pass to the center for an easy backdoor score.

Melissa and Rich jumped up and applauded. Two plays later, the ref called a block against Andrew.

Melissa yelled, "You're kidding. He never touched him."

Rich tugged at her sleeve and said in a high falsetto, "Not so loud."

At the half, Melissa turned to Rich, "I feel like I haven't seen you in years. How'd the meeting go with Donald?"

Rich rubbed his hand down his face. "As 'The Donald' would say, 'This is war, and right now we're holding on to the hill, but if our new strategy doesn't work, instead of routing the enemy, we'll be in full retreat.'"

Melissa laughed. "'Apocalypse Now' meets the lingerie business?"

"Something like that, but actually that was the easiest part of the day yesterday. First thing yesterday morning I got a speeding ticket from some Junior G-man cop. Then we're missing three thousand *Slimmies* from the DC. We had to express some in for this order today."

"Well, if you want to find the *Slimmies*, look for the resident masochist. Who else would take three thousand garments designed to reduce your blood flow and your breathing capacity by half?" Melissa put her hand on her stomach as she spoke.

"Speaking of reduced blood flow, particularly to the brain, any movement from the guys at Sewell & Prather?" Rich asked.

"A rustle, maybe. Thomas called and countered with 5,000 less shares of stock and $10,000 more in cash. But I get the feeling that they are getting antsy.

I'm wondering what's really going on. Then on top of that, I've got this Harrell guy being a pain in the rear."

"That's not your only problem. You better watch out." Rich puffed out his chest. "Rita Sue Fox wants me. She was in Boston yesterday still playing that same sad song."

"You tell Rita Sue to go find her own logistics guy." Melissa hooked her arm through his. "Speaking of those poor children though, you know Kelly hasn't forgotten about that newscast. She's planning on watching the tape with you tomorrow."

"I guess it wouldn't do for me to tell her to take a number." Rich put his hand over Melissa's.

"About as much good as it would do to tell the wind not to blow."

"If I had six hours to chop down a tree, I'd spend four hours sharpening the ax."

— *Abraham Lincoln*
  - Posted on the Stabler cafeteria bulletin board in Charlotte, March

CHAPTER THIRTEEN

Images of hunched Indonesian children flitted across the television screen. Each bearing the weight of their family invisibly on their shoulders.

"See Dad, what did I tell you? Look at those poor kids. It's disgusting." Kelly's auburn ponytail bounced up and down through the back of her Carolina Panthers' hat as she pointed to the television.

"True enough, Kelly, but where do you think they'd be if they didn't have a job? You've got to realize these kids are feeding their families. Do you know what the average yearly income for an Indonesian family is?"

"No, but that's beside the point." Kelly crossed her arms and smirked at her father.

"No, that is not beside the point at all. Corporations can help develop a country, but if they go in overnight and change the standard of living dramatically, it would be a disaster. Before you decide how awful this is—and I am not saying that those kids are getting a great deal—but before you jump to conclusions on this issue, you need to do some more research."

"Like, I don't think so." Kelly rolled her eyes. "Pah-leez, Dad, this is not school."

"Hey, Kel, that's true, but you can't go throwing accusations around without the facts. Unless, of course, you're going into politics." Rich seemed to enjoy his joke more than anyone else. "So you come back and tell me the yearly income of Indonesian families and ten other facts about the quality of life there including something about housing. Then we'll talk."

Kelly sighed loudly. "But Dad—"

"But Dad, nothing. You're drawing conclusions from one side of the story. That doesn't make sense. You want to give me a hard time? Then you'd better get your facts straight.

"It's a given that life in Indonesia is more difficult than it is here in the States. Thinking that one thing makes it that way is naive. Get the facts before you solve the problem. If I solved problems at work before I knew what the story was, you'd be looking for work yourself."

Rich thought he was beginning to sound like his father. Kelly's next statement confirmed that.

"I know, I know, and you had to walk five miles in the snow to go to school. Fine, Dad. We'll just see who laughs last." Kelly sailed from the room flipping her ponytail. Rich imagined this was to emphasize her disgust at being the daughter of a cretin such as himself.

Melissa raised her eyebrows in Rich's direction.

"Why are you looking at me that way?" He asked.

"No reason in the world. Have I mentioned that her guidance counselor called and asked about us chaperoning the senior prom at the high school?" Melissa said.

Rich tried to roll his eyes and toss his head at the same time. "Like, I don't think so."

Melissa laughed.

"By the way, how do you think she does that wierd thing with her eyes?" Rich asked.

• • • • • • • • •

At the initial meeting of the Whitehead Service Team on Monday, everyone acted like a freshman at their first high school dance. The group that gathered around the conference room table kept looking around at what everyone else did, wondering who would be the first to move.

Valerie Wagner bustled in with handouts and passed them around the room. She knew from prior experience that this could be a dangerous time in the team process. Valerie surveyed the group that, with the exception of Marcus, John and Raymond, was relatively quiet.

Quiet was poison. Too much watch-and-listen mentality could cause a team to stall. Valerie knew that from experience. The GOH Team had almost died a slow agonizing death, punctuated by the nervous coughing of its members, until an off-site lunch helped push a hole in the log jam of the group's silence. Valerie's mission was to give everyone a clear understanding of how the teaming process operated. She hoped her spiel would encourage people to speak up.

• • • • • • • • • •

Israel Stanley sat, blowing air through a paper clip, keeping his eyes on the legal pad in front of him. Rachel, his boss, sat next to him. Rachel really wanted him on this team and he respected Rachel. She listened pretty well when you talked to her, but you had to be sort of careful about giving her bad news. She tended to associate you with the news you gave her. Once when Israel told her that several of the other customer service reps needed more training, she dogged him for the next two weeks about everything he did. He thought she must be having a bad time outside of work and he was a convenient target for her nervous energy. Still, he tried not to make anymore career-limiting remarks, "CLRs," as the other customer service reps called them. It didn't help when they ended up having to fire two of the people he tried to talk to her about, both times after major screw-ups with clients. That disappointed Israel because he thought at least one of the reps was a keeper who lacked phone training. Still, Israel tried to be optimistic. Maybe this new team would help.

• • • • • • • • • •

Larry Adams pushed back in his chair. This kind of thing was such a waste of his time. Donald Stabler needed to get his head screwed on straight. The finance function was swamped and he was sitting in some meeting with everyone from Rich, Donald's latest golden boy from logistics, to that designer from sales and marketing. Geez, was she a flake.

Donald had told him to cooperate, but he wondered if this sort of stuff wasn't a grand scheme on Rich's part to take over his job or get Rich a higher head count at finance's expense. That's all right, Larry thought, I'm not saying anything. I'll figure out his game and head him off at the pass. This team stuff is only a smoke screen.

• • • • • • • • • •

Rich noticed that the configuration around the conference room table served as an easy map to the areas represented. First, there were Rachel and Israel from the customer service area. Rich and Rachel had picked Israel since his job involved constant telephone contact and problem solving with Whitehead and other customers. Next to Rachel sat Nandy Gamble from marketing and sales who looked like a Cyclops, one of her eyes covered by hair. Beside her, sat her boss, Marcus Warren, who represented the sales perspective on the Whitehead Service Team. Today he wore a silk Italian suit and a sort of macho-cool attitude like Don Johnson on an old episode of 'Miami Vice.'

John O'Connor from manufacturing sat next to Marcus, and Raymond Rodriquez from planning sat next to John. Today's one-up discussion between Raymond and Marcus took place back and forth across the front of John, occasionally involving him. Valerie caught various pieces of the conversation. Raymond and Marcus had moved past their discussion from the last meeting on coffee and on to cigars.

Raymond, an avid reader of 'Cigar Aficionado,' stated that he rarely smoked anything but handrolled Cuban cigars.

"How can you do that?" Marcus said. "They're illegal."

"I have my connections. If I get in a bind I'll smoke one from the Dominican Republic, an Avo or an A. Fuente Opus X."

Marcus lifted his shoulders slightly and tossed back his comment. "I've got to tell you, Raymond, the Cuban brands that I've smoked seem to me to be mediocre at best."

Raymond lifted his shoulders to return the volley of 'Yuppie Superiority' that Marcus had lobbed his way.

"Hey, you've got to know your source. There's a lot of guys out there selling Cuban cigars that have never been within a hundred miles of Cuba." Raymond laughed. "They're counterfeits."

The discussion ended as the group was called to order. Bob Ketchum, sitting next to Raymond, actually had the last word on cigars.

"I swear it is little Beamer-driving, wet-behind-the-ears, know-it-alls like you two that drive the price of a cigar up so high the rest of us can't enjoy one. Used to, I could get me a really fine cigar for two, three bucks. Now it's five or six bucks if I'm lucky."

Larry Adams turned to Bob. "Hey Bob, don't hold back, tell us how you really feel." Larry and Denise Burton from IT, along with Rich, rounded out the

Valerie introduced herself and said, "I think most of you know each other, but I'd like for all of you to introduce yourselves and explain your function here at Stabler."

Rachel started. "I'm Rachel Alvarado. I'm responsible for customer service. I work closely with both distribution and manufacturing to see that we satisfy our customers, both in the quality of our distribution and the quality of our manufacturing."

"I'm Israel Stanley. I work on the front lines, talking to customers every day, mostly when they are unhappy. Along the way, I've managed to acquire a new vocabulary." He smiled. "Not all of which can be used in public." Despite his tie, Israel looked a bit rumpled. His shirt sleeves seemed to creep up his arms as if the sleeves were too short or his arms too long.

Nandy Gamble brushed her jet black hair out of her face long enough for the others to see her missing eye. "I'm Nandy Gamble. I'm a designer in the sales and marketing area."

"I'm Marcus Warren from the sales area. I just try to keep Nandy in the road." Marcus adjusted a lapel on his suit.

"I'm John O'Connor. I head the Lexington plant, and with Raymond's help, I try like hell to figure out what Marcus and Nandy want." John gestured to Raymond on his right.

"I'm Raymond Rodriquez from planning where our goal is to stay one step ahead of marketing and sales. They produce new SKUs like they're rabbits."

"Larry Adams, I'm vice president of the finance area at Stabler." Rich noticed that Larry had worn a red and yellow power tie that matched his red and yellow suspenders. Larry didn't have quite the macho to pull off the suspenders so he looked like 'GQ' meets 'Revenge of the Nerds.'

"I'm Denise Burton. I head the Information Technology area under Larry. I'm very excited about what our new computer system will do for manufacturing and distribution."

"I'm Bob Ketchum. I run the Distribution Center here in Charlotte." He pointed at Denise. "That is until the new computer system takes over."

"I'm Rich Morrison. I try to lead the logistics area. Every now and then it follows me. Other times I've got to run to catch up with it."

Rich made eye contact one by one with each potential team member as

Rich made eye contact one by one with each potential team member as he spoke, "I want you all to know up front that if after today's orientation meeting, you feel the Whitehead Service Team isn't right for you, there is a no-fault 'I don't think so' clause in our agreement."

John O'Connor leaned over to Bob. "I'm going to stay on no matter what. Maybe it'll get Walter off my back about this team stuff. You guys may as well have created cold fusion over here to hear him tell it."

Rich found that interesting in light of Walter's constant haranguing about the teaming process in Charlotte. So far, Donald had held Walter in check, but Rich wasn't sure how much longer that would last.

Valerie Wagner finished handing out the last of her papers. The silver pin that she wore today covered most of her lapel. It was a big apple with miniatures of various New York landmarks such as the Empire State Building and the Statue of Liberty hanging from the bottom. The landmarks swayed slightly as she spoke.

Valerie began the meeting with a review of the team process. "As John just noted, many of you have tried teams in various forms over the last ten years. After a lot of trial and error, what we've found here in Charlotte is that teaming as a program fails, but teaming as a process works."

"Why is that?" John said, with a smirk similar to the one Raymond had worn earlier during the discussion on cigars.

"It's because we are involving many people and we're aware of where teams are in the stages of teaming and, finally, we believe that the process ebbs and flows. Changes shapes and evolves. We don't have one set of teams that will stay the same forever. We have teams that come together with a purpose, a very clear purpose that we call a charter and once they fulfill their charter they disband. No need to have a group unless you have a purpose to that group."

"I'll agree with that. Too many meetings as it is." John's smirk changed to a slight frown.

"So teaming is a very fluid process. Your team will be supported by a liaison from our Leadership Team here in Charlotte. Also, our Communication Team which, as we speak, is working on getting out the word about the challenge of change, will assist you. For those of you who aren't familiar with the teaming process, let me give you a quick run down on team etiquette. If you'll look at the first page of the handout I gave you, you'll see the five points of team etiquette listed:

1. You may not send someone else in your place to the team meeting. For the team to succeed, we need you here.

2. Every team member should be punctual and all meetings will begin and end on time. Normally, teams meet for an hour. This limits the constraint on your time and allows you to really focus on the meeting.

3. No telephone calls or interruptions during team meetings. Beepers are turned off.

4. Within the team, there are no supervisors or ranking. All team members are equal.

5. Team members will not seek to win an argument. Team members should balance advocacy and inquiry, and should speak candidly, openly and clearly, and listen actively.

"Any questions?" Valerie looked around the room.

"We're not all in the same location. What if I can't afford the travel time?" Raymond asked.

"That's not a problem. We can arrange to have conference calls to include other locations," Valerie replied.

She pointed at the page in her hand. "If you look at the bottom of page one you'll see the six rules of our team. These are designed to encourage trust, openness and participation. The team rules are:

1. Total honesty. This process will not be effective if you don't say what you think. No politics, no games and no adversarial relationships. You're here because your views and beliefs are important.

2. Total amnesty. There will be no repercussions back to individuals for things said at team meetings. The minutes will not contain individual beliefs and views. This is not because we want a veil of secrecy, but because we want people to be totally honest without fear of negative reactions/repercussions.

3. Listen to others. Actively listen to others and be aggressive in trying to understand what others are saying. Listen for both the facts and the feelings

behind what people are saying. Make eye contact, minimize listening distractions and paraphrase back to the speaker what you are hearing.

4. Stay focused. Your team is charged with an awesome and exciting responsibility. Stay on the agenda topics and make sure your comments contribute to the discussion at hand.

5. Manage time. Team meetings will run as scheduled, sixty minutes or less. Once you're used to dealing with sixty-minute meetings, the team becomes more effective and efficient.

6. Be prepared. At the end of each meeting, assignments will be made. Team members are responsible for completing assignments on schedule. Both the team leader and the team liaison will support you in completing assignments.

"Our meetings are action-oriented." Valerie pointed to the second page of the handout. "On the second page of your handout is a typical team meeting agenda."

The second page began:

A. Assign recorder.

B. Review meeting rules.

C. Review Model of Success.

D. Review last meeting.

E. Pursue objectives.

F. Review assignments.

Valerie continued as the others looked at the page. "The first four items should take us two to five minutes. The last item should take two to five minutes. So you see, the majority of our meeting time should be spent pursuing the meeting objectives. None of us needs another meeting added to our schedule. We know that each of you has a very harried workday with little time for wide-open thought time. So our meetings are meant to be thought-provoking, giving you some sit-back-and-think time, but also short enough so that they don't waste time. Look at this as a chance to have our own thought process enhanced by what others say. A chance to break open the mold."

"I think that may be our problem. A couple of people like O'Connor over there already broke the mold," Bob said pointing at John with his pencil.

"Hey, at least I can keep up with my inventory," John shot back, referring to the lost *Slimmies.*

Valerie ignored them. "Now we also know the reality is, sometimes teams get stuck. One way we have to deal with this is a team evaluation. The evaluation forms in your packets can be used to track our meetings' progress. These forms are an easy way to evaluate how the team spent our time. From time to time someone may be asked to play the role of team assessor."

Valerie then reviewed the last sheet of the group's handout that explained role descriptions for the Team Sponsor, Team Liaison, Team Leader, Team Reporter, Team Recorder and Team Member:

A **Team Sponsor** is the person who defines the need for a team. The sponsor sells the idea of the team to the Leadership Team. They may also write the team charter's first draft. They may become a team leader, liaison or a team member, or they may have finished their involvement with the team once they help define its mission.

A **Team Liaison** provides direction for a team as it pursues its charter. The liaison, who is also a member of the Leadership Team, monitors the team to see that it is true to the teaming process and that it is making progress on its charter. The liaison is not a member of the team and should only be involved in support of the team leader, in assuring the team's focus on its charter and in responding to questions from the team. The liaison has the authority to speak for the Leadership Team. In responding to questions from the team the liaison has three options. He or she may agree for the team to move forward, may not agree for the team to move forward and will explain the reasons why, or will respond in a week's time to a question they are unsure of after they have consulted the Leadership Team.

The **Team Leader**'s task is to obtain real team performance. To make sure that the team's synergy causes its performance to be greater than the contribution of its members. The team leader walks a narrow path because they must ensure quality communication and participation, run meetings, provide focus on the Model of Success and the team charter, build commitment, grow team members, manage team boundaries, and accept responsibility for team growth and progress, while at the same time being an active team member. A team member whose ideas and opinions are no more important than any other team member's ideas.

The **Team Reporter** is a role that changes from month to month. The reporter is spokesperson for the team at the monthly Communication Forum. This brings a sense of urgency to the role. The reporter wants progress, closure and action so that when they stand up to report they will have several significant things to say regarding their team's progress.

The role of **Team Recorder** is assigned at the beginning of each meeting and should be rotated around to all the team members except the team leader. The obvious role of the team recorder is to take the minutes of the team meetings. These minutes serve as a thread of consistency from meeting to meeting. They include the date, time, location, attendees, topics discussed, decisions made, assignments and call for the next meeting. This involves everyone equally and emphasizes the 'level playing field' of the team. And, of course, requires that the team recorder really listens to what everyone is saying. Team recorders are not responsible for production and distribution of the minutes, they simply submit their minutes to the team leader who takes care of production and distribution.

What is the role of the **Team Member**? Team members are by nature a diverse group. They are commonly united in that each team member is a person who has agreed to be committed to the team, to work with the team and to work toward the team's success.

"Rich has written a charter for this team that the Leadership Team has already reviewed. Rich, you're on," Valerie said.

Valerie sat as Rich stood and passed around copies of the team charter. He read each item and thoroughly discussed it with the team, covering specifically their opportunity, the process, the Evidence of Success and the resources available to them.

"Seventy-two percent order fulfillment is not going to cut it anymore. This team must be committed to thinking and acting boldly. Everyone must leave behind their territories if we're going to redesign our distribution efforts," Rich emphasized.

"What if I don't like the things the team is doing?" Raymond asked.

"You don't have to agree with everything the team does, but you do have to support it," Rich said. "Otherwise we'd get nowhere fast."

Denise Burton presented the information on the new computer capabilities. Then she announced the on-site support people for the plant and the distribution center, Paula Orr and Charlie Patel, respectively.

The meeting ended with plans for a second meeting the next Monday. As the group began to get up from the table Rich said, "Don't forget, if you feel you can't commit to the team, please let me know by Wednesday."

● ● ● ● ● ● ● ●

In the hallway Nandy ran after Israel. Several times over the two years she'd worked at Stabler she'd considered sleeping with him, then changed her mind. Sometimes you just needed a guy for a friend.

"Israel—"

Israel turned back and waited for her to catch up with him. He shifted his legal pad and tugged at his wayward sleeve.

"So what did you think?" Nandy asked, putting her hand on Israel's arm. Shy guys were so cute.

"About what?" Israel stuttered slightly.

"That total amnesty bullshit. Are you going to tell them about your customer service ideas?"

"Are you kidding? Rachel stands a better chance of getting total amnesia than she does of following a total amnesty policy. You don't really think they mean it, do you?"

Nandy squeezed Israel's arm. "I guess we'll see."

"You better not take your eyes off the goal. If you do, what you see will scare the hell out of you."

— Bob Ketchum to Rich Morrison and Valerie Wagner, after a Stabler Leadership Team meeting, March

CHAPTER FOURTEEN

It started innocently enough. Nandy Gamble flipped her hair out of her eyes and announced, "I was thinking over the weekend. Wouldn't it be great if we came up with some stylish disposable panties? After all, they're making Depends in three different styles now. If we could get the design right, we might even get into, like, you know, stylish disposable boxers."

And then it was on. The second meeting of the Whitehead Service Team that next Monday became as loud and raucous as an old-fashioned revival meeting. People shouted back and forth across the table. At one point, Rich imagined that their words could have been, "Amen! Preach it, Brother!" Each shouter preached against their own idea of evil.

Nandy's words were barely out before Raymond's started.

"You can't be serious." He put his hands in front of him like he was a superhero bracing to stop a runaway train. "This is just the sort of thing that makes planning a living hell. We're still trying to figure out how to get your fanny-firming slip to market. And each product has a hundred different versions with a hundred different SKUs and you keep mutating them. You're crazy."

Nandy tossed her hair again, offering a brief glimpse of her eye. "Listen, I was hired to create and that's what I'm going to do. I can't help it if the rest of you take six years to get a product to market. What about the Wonderbra? They beat us, didn't they? I'd had that design for months. I'd been begging you people to get the bras out there, but nobody could do a thing."

"Now they've got a market share that we could only dream about," Marcus said in agreement.

Bob threw his hands up into the air. "Hello, we are sitting on enough of those bras to circle the Earth three times over. It's crazy."

"Well, we were told by Nandy and the marketing people that we wouldn't be able to produce the things fast enough," John O'Connor said, pulling himself up straighter in the chair as he spoke.

"And if they'd gone to market when I designed them, we wouldn't have. By the time we got our product out, everyone's cleavage had been pushed up for months." Nandy huffed.

Rich sighed. It all reminded him of the time when Andrew was three—he drank an entire can of Coke and ran in circles for two hours—going nowhere—but boy did he get there fast. I need to get them focused, Rich thought.

More discussion broke out like bits of enemy sniper fire, erratic bursts from the most unpredictable spots.

Rich waved his hands to get everyone's attention. *This isn't going to be an easy team.*

"I hate to break up a good discussion, but I think what we need to do is focus on our goal. The goal of absolutely knocking-the-socks-off, taking-no-prisoners, amazing and delighting the Whitehead company. As far as we're concerned, we want Whitehead to think of us as the ninth wonder of the world." Rich turned. "Rachel, what does the Whitehead chain want that we're not giving them now?"

"One of the biggest problems is our slow order fulfillment. I have stores begging me, not only for their orders, but for any word on when the orders might possibly ship."

"So tell us something we don't know. We have a molasses ship schedule and we communicate by smoke signals," Raymond said.

"Only after we start the fire by rubbing two sticks together. So you could say that, yes," Rachel replied.

"Well, for the millionth time, I can't ship what I don't have," Bob said.

"And for the zillionth time, I can't snap my fingers and have the little production elves make the garments instantly. They're still working for the cookie people," John said.

"Sounds like we need to get some feedback on how to improve communication with Stabler, first. That should be the fastest fix," Larry said.

"Manufacturing's another story."

"So, Rachel, will you and Denise get us a complete picture of the communication process with Stabler and where that breaks down?" Rich asked.

Both women nodded.

"I'm not trying to be obstinate. I think everyone here sees that if we had the information on what is selling in real time and if we can figure out a way to shorten our product runs, then we could cut out a lot of our obsolete stock and excess inventory. That is a mighty big 'if' as far as I'm concerned," John said.

"We've got to start somewhere, John. How about you and Raymond educating us on what is involved in changing manufacturing over from one product to the other? Look to see if there are ways to shorten the time it takes to change the line from one product to the other so that we can respond more rapidly to demand."

"I don't see how we're going to be able to do more than we're doing," John commented.

"Well, somebody's figured it out. Customization is killing us. Everybody in the market can give you anything you want yesterday and we can't give it to you next month," Bob said.

"I'm telling you, it's very stifling to my creative juices to have no hope of ever seeing my designs on the market." For emphasis, Nandy slung her hair out of her eyes again. "What good does it do to think out of the box if you people are not going to be provocative?"

"I believe that is proactive." Valerie corrected her.

"Whatever." Nandy's eyebrow, the one that was visible, raised in seemingly unconcerned agreement.

"All that aside. How has the Whitehead account changed?"

Marcus spoke up. "They have a lot less storage because they are in the high-dollar malls. They want instant replenishment, and like all our accounts, they carry every style of lingerie you can imagine. Women and men are becoming a lot more adventurous in the styles of underwear they buy."

Marcus continued, shaking his Mont Blanc pen for emphasis. "One of my big concerns is quality. Can someone not get a handle on this quality stuff before we're all working for one big quality department?"

"We have an in-house team looking at that. Trying to streamline the process," Rich noted.

Marcus continued. "It seems like nine times out of ten, if Bob tells me we've got a ship problem, it's a quality issue. It's like 'Invasion of the Body Snatchers' or a vampire movie or something. They're everywhere. Going to take over the world. Soon everybody will be a quality guy out at night looking for fresh human blood."

"Well, actually, Marcus, that is what we're hoping." Rich smiled. "Not the human blood part, but everyone paying attention to quality."

"Well, we've already done quality circles and that didn't seem to work. So what'll it be this time, quality squares?" John chimed in. "I suppose it's one of you distribution genius's other breakthroughs."

Everyone smiled as Valerie said, "Good idea, John, glad you thought of it. Really, though, Rich is right. The Quality Team's new charter says they will figure out a way for everybody to be in quality- so that nobody is in quality."

"Makes perfect sense to me," Marcus said.

Valerie smiled. "I'm not ignoring that issue, but I think we should look back at Rich's original question—how can we improve for the customer, above and beyond just working on problems? Israel, do you have any thoughts?"

"I think the communication issue is key. If we had information at our fingertips to give to a field rep when we're trying to sell to customers, that would help," Israel said.

"What kind of information?" John asked.

Israel thought for a second before he answered. "I'm talking about beyond whether we had stuff in stock. Though that would be nice. Instead of pushing these losing items that have no market, maybe we could help analyze their current inventory and get them to make more intelligent decisions. How much floor space to allocate to different SKUs and things like that. We'd smoke the competition."

"I've been trying to tell that to Donald and Walter for years." Larry bristled. "They won't buy it."

"I think they will, Larry. The alternatives aren't that special," Rich said. "Denise, what would it take to get that kind of program up and running? Will this new software do it?"

"Yes and no. We'd have to modify it for our field reps and ..." Denise sighed loudly, "that might take some doing."

In other words, it's butt-kissing time, Rich thought. The tekkies in IT already thought the place was theirs for the taking.

"We'd need some specs as to what you want, then we'll tell you if it's possible. We're not out in the field every day," Denise said.

Marcus jumped in. "I'll have my people together and we'll give you everything you need to know by next week. If I do that, can I expect to get something out of you guys?"

"Marcus, have we ever told you no?" Larry asked.

"More times then I can count, big guy."

"Hold up, guys." Nandy shook her hands as if she was trying to dry nail polish. Rich had seen Kelly do it many times, flopping her hand over at the wrist and shaking her fingers. Nandy's black fingernail polish had bits of silver in it that reflected the light as she moved. Different made the world go round, Rich reminded himself.

"Israel has programming experience, don't you, Israel?" Nandy's question had an emphatic tone to it.

The mention of his name seemed to startle Israel.

"Only a little bit," he said.

"Yeah, but enough. So with what you know about customer service—you being the one talking to the field reps every day—couldn't you work on that with IT? Help pound the code out and save some mega time." Nandy persisted.

If you could get past that black fingernail polish, Nandy had good thoughts in there among her off-the-wall approaches to everything, Rich thought.

Denise tapped her pen on the table in front of her. "That won't be necessary, really."

Bob Ketchum came alive. "I'm just a low-tech distribution guy, but it makes sense to me."

Still Denise resisted. "I think we're smart enough to talk with Marcus and get the job done. Don't you think so, Larry?"

Larry pushed his lips in and out several times. "Well, sure."

Marcus joined in. "Come on, Larry. You guys are always talking about how buried you are. I trust Israel to know the scoop. If it'll make you feel any better, one of my guys will sit in."

"I'd have to agree with Marcus," Rich said. What a great opportunity to shake up the IT self-image.

Valerie nodded her agreement.

Rich continued, "You guys still have a customs program to do for Irving. Rachel, can you cover Israel's stuff?"

Rachel folded her arms. "Rich, I'm already two short in my head count. I can spare him, but not for some year-long project."

"If you're short, Rachel, hire somebody." Raymond said.

"Thank you, Raymond. But as you well know, it's difficult to find someone who can hit the ground running, and Israel is really quite good at what he does."

• • • • • • • • •

Looking down at his pad, Israel had to smile at his boss's words. She could rake him over the coals every day, yet get her in a meeting like this, and she made it sound as if he had arrived on the wings of an angel, fresh from customer service heaven.

Israel wasn't all that anxious to work with Denise. Every time he'd suggested any changes to the database program, she'd bit his head off and told him in no uncertain terms why it wasn't possible.

Israel listened as the majority of the team agreed that he was the natural choice to help Denise and the IT people.

He couldn't help but notice that Denise crossed her arms and never looked his way again for the rest of the meeting.

After the meeting, Nandy walked down the hall with him. Israel could never decide if her interest in him was personal or not. Today, he didn't care.

He had planned to bide his time until he got the feel of this teaming thing. Now, thanks to Nandy who walked beside him as if she had springs in her shoes, he was right in the middle of some power thing with Rachel and IT, and no telling who else. The new program for customer service and field reps was important, but Israel didn't look forward to trying to write it with Denise. If he was lucky, maybe she'd slough it off on some underling.

Nandy punched him lightly on the arm. "See, I told you this teaming thing was going to be cool." The way she said the word cool, it came out as "cuuuUUL" with sort of a lilt at the end.

Oh, right, double cuuuUUL, he thought.

• • • • • • • • • •

After the meeting, Rich sat down with Bob to look over the recommendations of the GOH Team.

They finished up just as Barbara announced that Melissa was on the line. Rich picked up the phone as Bob walked out the door.

"Thomas Sewell just called. I have forty-eight hours to decide on their offer. So what do you think, really? Yes or no?" Melissa's words tumbled out, running together. Rich had to take a minute to sort them out.

"I think I've lived with you long enough to say, 'Mmmmm—I don't know.'"

"Rich," Melissa said.

"Melissa, honey, I feel like you're having serious doubts. But then as I recall, Friday night at the game, Mr. Harrell had convinced you to sell."

"I know, I know, but I'm just not sure. And really, I've had worse clients than old Mr. Harrell. Besides, I'm not going to let some old windbag push me around. I know I'm right and he knows I'm right. His attorney called this morning to try and settle the bill."

"You sent him on to Frank's office, didn't you?" Rich asked. Frank Tufano handled legal issues for AdWorks and the Morrison's personal legal affairs.

"No, I suddenly acquired a law degree and handled it myself. Sometimes—"

"Okay, okay. Dumb question."

"What I can't figure out is why is Sewell & Prather in a rush all of a sudden? Sort of makes me want to drag my feet." Melissa sighed. "Where's my crystal ball when I need it?"

"You know how I feel about that. When in doubt, throw it out. You're the intuitive one in the family. Remember me, I'm just the cave dweller. The offer's in order. Frank's looked it over. He thinks it looks good. I think it looks good. You're still dragging your feet. What do you think that means?"

"I think it means it's time for me to hang up before we fight about what I'm supposed to do. Then I'll call back and see if Barbara will give me your voice mail. I'll leave you a message about what I decide I'm going to do. How's that sound to you?"

"If you don't want advice, why do you ask for it?" Rich had enough going on without this. Melissa needed to make up her mind.

"Don't hang up mad," she said.

"I'm not mad. I've got to go. Leave me that message." Rich hung up the phone, shaking his head.

At AdWorks, Melissa put the phone in its cradle and sat back in her chair trying to remember the last time she had felt this unsettled.

Later, Rich checked his voice mail only to discover that Melissa had turned down the Sewell & Prather offer.

Go figure.

GOOSE CHASE

"Sometimes you see things that make you really worry what's going on with the management in this place."

"Hey, at least, they're thinking. My brother-in-law got laid off last week for the third time over at Rigsbee Manufacturing. This Rich character can get on your nerves, but at least he ain't got his head buried in the sand."

"From what I hear, the boss over in quality wishes he could bury him."

— Conversation on the Stabler packaging line between Luke Sullivan and Billy Boyton after changes in quality procedures were rolled out, March

CHAPTER FIFTEEN

Two weeks later in the Leadership Team meeting, Rachel and her team presented their 'change' commercial. In the manner of an old-fashioned vaudeville show, a young woman curtseyed to the audience and then placed a sign on an easel at the side of the room. In red block letters it said, "THE FUZZY BUZZIES." Blue fuzzy characters danced into the room to the tune of "You Always Hurt The One You Love." The blue fuzzy suits had holes cut out for each buzzy's face, which had been covered with blue make-up. The creatures wore stocking caps in different colors and had block lettered signs pinned to the front and back of their costumes. The red-capped creature was TQM, the green-capped creature was REENGINEERING, the purple-capped creature was JIT, the orange-capped creature was EMPOWERMENT, and lastly, yellow-capped triplets were TRAIN, TRAIN and TRAIN. The Fuzzy Buzzies bumped into one another blindly, pushing the hoops that rounded their costumes out, this way and that. Whirling and bumping until eventually each dancing 'buzz word' bit the dust. The last, TQM, did a swan-like move, then melted into the floor, his blue belly protruding up like the hump of a whale, his TQM sign balancing across the top.

Then a young man appeared, bowed from the waist and put another sign on the easel. This one read, "THE PERSISTENT PRINCIPLES." Through the door tumbled a group of gymnasts, each wearing a different color warm-up. Instead of wearing their block-lettered signs, they carried them, each pausing in front of the easel to put down his sign and take a bow. The red gymnast was RESPONSIVENESS, the blue was TRUST, the green was OBJECTIVITY, the yellow was TEAMWORK, the purple was METHODICAL, the orange was INNOVATION, and the black was PRACTICAL.

To the tune of "Stayin Alive," the gymnasts performed intricate routines for several minutes. Each routine depended on proper timing and integration of their efforts. METHODICAL, INNOVATION, PRACTICAL and TEAMWORK formed a bottom layer on their hands and knees. TRUST and OBJECTIVITY hopped on top of this foundation, and with both of them securely in place, RESPONSIVENESS jumped on top. With his place secured, RESPONSIVE-NESS stood and pulled two checkered victory flags from his pocket and waved them above his head.

Great, Rich thought, Donald will love the racing reference.

The music switched to The Beatles singing, "Changes," and the pyramid magically disappeared and reformed, again with RESPONSIVENESS standing on top waving the victory flags. This was repeated once more before the music faded and the gymnasts formed a line to take a bow. Applause from the audience revived the Fuzzy Buzzies, who also took a bow, hamming up their part by continuing to try and bump one another out of the way with their big hooped bellies.

Valerie stood after the applause died down. "That's a tough act to follow, so I won't even try. I'm passing around a rough draft of the items and a brief description of the things that I think should be included in this Personal Path Forward kit. I want you to look at it and think about what other things we might include and things you think don't belong or need further work. Remember, our objective with this is to give each employee tools to use in shaping their destiny."

The group read and commented on Valerie's draft.

"So what exactly will we do with these two new creations?" Irving wanted to know.

"It is important that we use them as effectively as possible. To mark the beginning and to set people's focus in the right direction. The Communication Team would like to present the Fuzzy Buzzies and the Persistent Principles at the next Communication Forum.

"We also believe it is very important that we have some immediate feedback. Maybe we can have white boards posted for people to write their suggestions or thoughts. We're wide open to any ideas you guys have on getting folks to push the envelope instead of lick it."

"I'm very concerned that people know about the Personal Path Forward kits. We can promote them at the Communication Forum and I can send out a memo, but I wish there was something else we could do," Denise said.

"People are not going to be very excited about this, you know. There are a lot of people who remember the good ol days," Bob said. "Besides, you've got to remember we've done some of this before. People tune you out."

"Now, Bob, you and I both know that the good ol days weren't so good, and even if they were, they're not coming back. The focus for everyone at Stabler should be, how can I add value to the company? And can I be happy doing that? If you can't answer the first, maybe the Personal Path Forward kit is for you. If you can answer the first, but the answer to the second is no—you won't be happy adding value—then maybe you need to think about a career somewhere else." Rich said.

"But people get afraid, don't they?" Irving asked.

"Believe me, Irving, I understand that. I'm dreaming about *Slimmies* at night. And there are plenty of days I feel like I've got a target on my back. The trick is to help people see that change is inevitable. They can set a sail and use the wind of change or they can be blown about wherever it might take them. That's their choice," Rich said.

Rachel seemed very excited. "I think that the Communication Team could come up with a poster campaign to promote the Personal Path Forward kit. Something to tie in with the 'change' posters."

Within weeks, the Communication Team presented their posters for the Personal Path Forward kits. They were two feet by three feet with MASTERS OF DESTINY written in large purple letters across the top. The text read, "Don't be a timid employee any longer. Become a MASTER OF DESTINY." The text was superimposed over a picture of a Viking man and woman sitting side by side at a conference room table. "Get your Personal Path Forward kit today. Action figures are available upon request. Collect all six."

When the videotaped Fuzzy Buzzies and Persistent Principles reached Boston, Donald called Rich.

"Great work. Be sure and tell your Leadership Team that I like it. A real barn burner, as we used to say back in the Midwest. I like the take-no-prisoners attitude you've got going down there, Rich. "

It always worried Rich when he and Donald started using the same phrases. "I just hope we don't kill our own with 'friendly fire,' Donald."

No question, change was in the air. No question, not everyone was happy about it.

• • • • • • • • •

Rita Sue Fox crossed her legs and leaned back onto the couch.

"When I got your call, I thought to myself, now how can I help out Rick? He's been so sweet to me."

"Rich," Bev hissed under her breath from her place beside Rita Sue Fox.

"Rich, yes, Rich." Rita Sue smiled at Rich and Melissa. "Well, I said to myself, I'll just go down there and help his son with this project."

Bev hissed. "Daughter—"

"Daughter," Rita Sue said as if it were an original idea.

"Really, Rita Sue, that wasn't necessary." Rich said.

"Oh no, we had to reshoot down here anyway. So we really just stopped by on our way to work." Rita Sue acted as if it were nothing to swing by for a "little chat," as she called it.

Rich shook his head and looked at Melissa. Just days ago, Kelly had sat in the spot Rita Sue now occupied. Actually, Kelly had sort of bounced up and down on the couch.

She had said, "Dad, you won't believe it. My social studies teacher is going to let me do this 'Life in Indonesia' thing as my term project. Only I'm going to do part of it on the protest over factory conditions there. Do you think you could get Rita Sue Fox to talk to me?"

"I really hate to get more involved with that woman than I have to. Isn't there some other way you could do this project?"

"Daaaadddddd! Pah-leez!" Kelly had looked down her nose at her father.

"So I take that to be a no."

All he asked for when he called Bev was a ten-minute phone interview with Rita Sue. Kelly wanted to ask a few questions. Instead, that request had gotten turned around and twisted, and now Rita Sue sat on the couch looking every inch the lingerie crusader that she was. "Lifestyles of the Rich and Famous" was playing in his living room. All I need, Rich thought, is for her to call a press conference on my front steps and my life and career will be complete.

The door bell rang and Rich jumped off the couch. He had only thought about the press and now they were here. Unless, maybe, it was Robin Leach.

When he opened the door, J. Thomas Sewell stood smiling at him. Okay, Rich thought, so it wasn't the press or Robin Leach, but it was hardly much better.

He tried to think of ways to keep Thomas Sewell out on the front step. "We've got leprosy, all under quarantine." Or, "Mad Cow disease has struck." Anything to keep him out of the house. Melissa had made her decision, Rich understood that to mean that Thomas, who was standing there trying his best to peer around Rich, was out of their lives.

"Hi, Rich," Thomas said. "I was in the neighborhood and thought I'd touch base with Melissa."

Rich smiled tightly and said nothing. What part about 'no' had Thomas misunderstood?

"I'm not interrupting anything, am I?" Thomas leaned around again.

"No, Thomas, come on in." Rich stepped aside.

"Rita Sue Fox, I can't believe this." Thomas was in the living room in two strides.

Certainly, the stretch limo out front wasn't a clue, Rich thought. What had he done that these two people wouldn't get out of his life? He felt like the Pharaoh when the plagues descended on him. He just wished he knew how many more he had to endure.

Was Thomas the frogs or the locusts?

"Hey, just like my mama used to tell me, 'Just cause you're sitting in the hen house, don't make you a chicken.'"

— Mike Fulton talking at the Ram's Head bar to his co-workers from Stabler about a new training program, March

CHAPTER SIXTEEN

"So what you're saying is that you want me to do my job and everyone else's too." Mike Fulton looked around the circle of guys and then back at Bob and Rich.

"No, what we're saying is that everyone is going to be able to work in any area of the warehouse," Bob said. "You'll get paid for what you know."

Rich spoke up. "What Bob is saying is that we have the technology now to direct the warehouse and plan the workflow, but what we need to respond to the market is for everyone in the warehouse to be able to roll with the workflow. Packers, sorters, shrink wrapping, GOH, everyone does everything. If we streamline our processes, everybody wins."

"You may call it streamlining, but I call it steamrolling," Mike said. "Besides, I'm no good at putting those little straps on the hanger."

"So most of the time you won't have to. You'll work where you do your best work. That makes sense for all of us, but if the customer needs something, we have got to make it happen," Rich said.

"How many times have we heard that? I mean it's a great idea and everything, but I just finished reading the new Quality Team charter. It looks to me like what you're trying to do is put a whole lot of people out of a job." Mike quickly shot back.

"No. That's not true. Nobody knows what their jobs will look like in six months, including me. We're creating new jobs. One way or the other, the old job won't exist. Either because we can't compete or because we chose to find a better way. Finding a better way means we create a new job, whereas not competing means we'll be out on the street looking for that new job," Rich said.

"Still it ain't what I was hired on for," Mike said. Several members of the group nodded their heads while others looked away wondering, no doubt, how they came to be standing next to Mike when he decided to get froggy with the boss. With the encouragement of the head-nodders, Mike continued. "And some people were wondering what exactly this secret Whitehead Service Team is all about."

Bob harrumphed. "Come on, Mike. For Pete's sake, you sound paranoid. There's nothing secret about the Whitehead Team."

"Yeah, well then, how come nobody from the floor is on it?"

"I'm on it." Bob's voice went up in pitch.

"So, your point is?" Mike asked.

"My point is, you've been working with me fifteen years now. Our kids graduated high school together, but all of a sudden I'm on a secret service team trying to screw you over?"

"Hey, I'm just telling you. I hear one of the customer service phone guys is on it, but we're not good enough," Mike said, looking around the circle to encourage support.

"For this being such a top secret team, you sure know a hell of a lot about it," Bob retorted.

Rich held up his hand. "Bob's not responsible for the team make-up. That was a decision of the entire Leadership Team based on my recommendations and then Mr. Stabler's approval. I'll be happy to look at it and consider Bob's recommendations of who to add from the floor, but you better know up front that this team's going to be intense.

"High pressure. Hit the ground running. No bellyaching about what you did or didn't get last year or how we've got to have a new snack vendor. We've got to kick butt and take names on this one." That sounded like a Donaldism, Rich thought. He made a note to poll the Leadership Team on the question of adding Mike to the Whitehead Service Team.

"Fine by me," Mike said. The men walked away still bunched together, stretching out and then retracting like an amoeba as they walked.

Bob turned to Rich. "Secret teams—that's a good one for you."

"Sounds like we need to get the Communication Team moving a little faster," Rich said. "Rumors like that'll kill you. Especially coming from a floor leader."

"Yeah, the guys do look up to him. Mike knows more about the dock than anyone we've got. It'd be nice if we could talk him into going along with this. But he's stubborn. You sure you want him on the team?" Bob asked.

"If we could talk him into believing in the team process, that would've happened by now. If you think he's the man, I don't see how we could lose by putting him on the team. He needs to see something happening."

One of the forklift drivers motioned to Bob. Even from a distance, Rich could see the color rise in Bob's face as he and the forklift driver began to talk. Rich watched as they became more and more animated. First pointing with their hands, Bob echoing the direction that the forklift driver pointed, then waving their arms for a minute or two until finally, Bob knocked the heal of his hand into his forehead like he'd just remembered to have a V-8. He turned and walked back toward Rich.

"Remember those 3,000 girdles that went AWOL?" Bob asked.

Rich nodded.

"Well, 5,000 pairs of men's designer boxer shorts decided to go on the lam with them."

"Are you sure?" Rich rubbed his neck trying to work out the kink that had started there a few minutes ago.

"Positive. Manuel told me that they were putting together an order for Rollins and were going to pull the last of the boxers to finish it off. No boxers."

"That's crazy. Are you sure he isn't mistaken?" Rich asked.

"I'll do some checking, but he's like Mike, one of the best we've got. If he says they're not here, then trust me—they aren't here," Bob said.

"Someone didn't just stroll out with those things under their jacket. There's some planning going into this."

Why did everything happen at once? Rich wished he could put up a sign that said: "PLEASE HOLD OFF ON SWIPING THE STOCK UNTIL WE GET THE WHITEHEAD SERVICE TEAM ON-LINE. THANK YOU FOR YOUR COOPERATION."

"What did your security guy find out about the *Slimmies?*" Rich asked as he and Bob began to walk back toward Rich's office.

"Not a damn thing, best I can tell. A lot of activity, but no results so far. I liked it better when that old guy Leonard was in charge of the on-site force."

Bob employed a third-party firm to oversee security for the Charlotte DC.

"I don't think I've met the new guy yet," Rich said.

"Name's Tony. He's okay. Just not as professional as Leonard."

"What happened to Leonard?" Rich asked.

"Got promoted to area operations. He deserved it. He's a good guy, always thinking of ways to give us more than we're paying for." Bob stopped walking. "But you know, Rich, this is a lot of product that we're missing here. Has to be more than one person involved. I can't figure out how they're getting them past the guys at the gate."

"You're right. Usually the U-Haul trailer is a tip-off for security." Rich said. "So what do you think we should do next?" Before Bob could answer, Rich added, "Have you checked the paperwork on the two orders to see if anything matches up?"

"That's what I'm thinking. I'll get Darla to pull it and see who handled both transactions. If I get a match I'll let you know," Bob said.

Rich hesitated. "Tell me this, how much do you trust the new guy in security?"

Bob took a moment to think about it. "I couldn't say. He acts like he wants to help."

"Who is your contact at Security Resources now?"

"Leonard has our area," Bob said.

"Maybe it's time you went back to him for some help. I hate to be suspicious, but like you said, there's more than one hand in the till on this one. Someone in the security area may be involved." The kink in Rich's neck seemed to ease up and then came back twice as strong before he could even move his hand.

"Yeah, may be," Bob murmured.

Valerie stood waiting for Rich and Bob in the reception area outside Rich's office.

"We need to talk." Her lips pressed together, forming a solid line that was flat and tight.

"I've got work to do." Bob started to excuse himself.

"It's okay, Bob, you might as well hear what happened." She waved at Bob like a traffic cop, her hand pointing him in the direction of Rich's office.

"I was just going to listen through the keyhole anyway." Bob smiled as he changed direction and headed into Rich's office.

"What happened?" Rich asked as he walked into the interior office. Not that he really wanted to know what happened, but it was his sworn duty somehow to listen. At least Valerie wouldn't be reporting a theft.

"We had a lunch-n-learn for the people who wanted to ask questions about the Personal Path Forward kits. It was horrible. I thought everyone would be excited about them, but a lot of people are angry. They think they're getting screwed." Valerie sank into a chair in Rich's office. "I'm at zero. I mean we worked so hard on those kits and if you could have seen how upset some people were. Then the written comments were anonymous. Geez, I'm surprised some of those questionnaires didn't spontaneously combust with what they had written on them."

"Don't they like the kit, or are they mad because they have to think about it?" Rich asked.

"I think it's because they have to think about it and the uncertainty. I know it's human nature to seek the sure thing. And here there is no sure thing," Valerie answered.

"Cheer up. Walter would tell you that Rome wasn't built in a day. Employees didn't become dependent overnight, and they won't become independent overnight, either."

"I lose patience. Instead of smiling and trying to explain it one more time, what I want to do is bite their heads off and tell them to get real."

"Everybody feels like that sometimes. And today, something you worked hard on got attacked. You'll even out. That's the kind of person you are." Rich shrugged. "Besides, every now and then, people do need to get told to get a life. If you have teenagers, they remind you to do that all the time."

"I want to feel sympathetic, but it's hard when you feel attacked." She paused, "I suppose they feel as much under attack as I do."

"That's right," Rich agreed. "But don't forget you're offering them some assistance in their war. And that in itself may turn the tide back again. It may entirely change the direction they're headed. Look for your victories. Study your losses, then forget them."

"Hey, Valerie, I'm not trying to be rude, but at least some people showed up. You got a lot of people out there on the line that have been told for years, 'Just do your job and we'll take care of you. Don't think. Thinking is for the big dogs.' Now they're getting told, 'Hey, we don't need you and we don't need your job. And thinking is not just for the big dogs anymore. Everybody gets to think.'" Bob's voice became louder with each sentence. "In fact, now instead of not thinking to keep your job, now you've got to think to keep your job. 'Oh, by the way, aren't you happy?'"

"But I didn't do that to them." Valerie shook her head at Bob.

"No, you didn't, but, hell, that doesn't make them any less mad. I'm just saying that it's no big surprise to me that people are steamed. And it sure as the devil ain't personal. They've got 'This Ain't My Jobitis.'"

"Well, Dr. Bob, what do you suggest as a cure?" Valerie edged her exasperated tone with a bit of a smile.

"Ask em if they would like to get a painful shot in their backside now or wait until the doc says he's got to cut off their arm to save em."

"Your eloquence never ceases to amaze me," Rich said.

"I don't know. I can try. Anything's possible . . . I suppose."

— Andrew Morrison responding to his basketball coach's request to play the guard position following another player's injury, March

CHAPTER SEVENTEEN

Rich couldn't decide whether Melissa was laughing or crying. Half-sobs punctuated the voice mail that she left him on Thursday afternoon. No one was hurt, Rich thought. If one of the children was hurt, Melissa would have said which hospital to meet her at. Maybe someone was dead. You wouldn't leave a dead message on the machine. Rich replayed the message. The second time around it sounded more like a semi-laugh.

"I can't believe it." Half-sob or semi-laugh. "I can't believe it." Half-sob or semi-laugh. "Call me."

He tried to think back to the morning but couldn't remember Melissa saying anything about a special meeting or something. Of course it wasn't like they'd had a long talk. They passed a couple of times in the hall and that was about it, with a quick kiss as he'd headed out the door.

When he called AdWorks, the administrative assistant told him that Melissa had run out for a few minutes. She asked if he wanted to leave a message. Rich hung up and tried Melissa's cell phone. As it rang, Rich thought about the predictions that new technology would have everyone working twenty-hour weeks by the 1990s. That was a laugh. For most people, the new technology just meant you could work more places, anywhere, anytime.

The phone quit ringing and an electronic voice said, "The cellular customer you are calling is not available at this time."

He spilled the diet Coke he was drinking when a breathless Melissa appeared in his office doorway, tears in her eyes and a big smile on her face.

"I tried you at the office and on your cell phone. Are you all right?" Rich wiped at the spot of diet Coke on his desk as Melissa shut the door.

Melissa nodded. "You won't believe it."

"I won't believe what?" Rich felt a tightening in his stomach. Was this going to be 'the new baby is on the way' announcement? On second thought, wouldn't that be an immaculate conception at this point in their lives?

"Sewell & Prather gave me everything I asked for. Everything."

"When? How?" Rich felt like jumping out of the chair and dancing on his desk. Instead, he grabbed Melissa and twirled her around and around across the thick off-white carpet.

"I don't know what happened," Melissa said, reaching up to kiss him, grazing his face with her lips. "Rich, if you don't stop, I'm going to throw up."

He stopped in mid-circle. "Can't have that. This is new carpet."

"I love a man with priorities." Melissa pushed her hair back behind her ears. "Thomas Sewell called not more than an hour ago. Said they'd meet everything I'd asked for before. Didn't even try to talk me down. Faxed me the new offer and even sent a runner over to Frank's with the original."

"So are you going to do it?" Rich hoped the answer was yes. However, that was only if the answer to the baby was no, but having learned a few lessons in nineteen years of marriage, he chose to keep this opinion to himself.

"Yes. Absolutely yes," Melissa kissed him again. "I've been looking for an answer and this one certainly came from above. The last word from Thomas was absolutely no more concessions. We were down to, 'take it or leave it.' And now this. I'm on my way to Frank's to sign some papers now."

"Wow—that's fast," Rich commented.

"Hey, hon, you've got to make hay while the sun shines."

Someone tapped on the door; it opened and Barbara stuck her head into the room. "I hate to interrupt, but Walter's on the line. I told him you're in conference, but he acts like the Russians are ready to push the button." Barbara looked at Melissa, waiting to be told whatever news Melissa had come all the way over to Stabler's to share.

"I've got to scoot anyway," Melissa said. She squeezed Rich's hand. "We can talk when you get home tonight."

Rich heard Melissa ask Barbara, "How's that new grandbaby of yours?" just before they shut his office door. It was shaping up to be a long day. He couldn't help but wonder what changed the minds of those guys over at Sewell & Prather. He pushed the button on the telephone speaker and said hello to Walter.

"Rich, listen. We've got a small problem. It looks like you've got some people who are helping themselves to whatever they want. What's going on down there?"

"Back it up, Walter, what are you talking about?" Rich asked, all thoughts of Sewell & Prather disappearing in an instant.

"The 5,000 pairs of boxer shorts that are gone, for one thing. We can't afford the amount of product shrinkage that you've got going on down there," Walter answered.

"Bob and I are dealing with it, Walter. That's all I can tell you. You know, it doesn't make me happy either."

"Maybe you should spend less time on your teams and more time on what we're paying you for," Walter said.

"Walter, you're paying me for solutions. I'm getting at them the best way I know how. Did Bob call you about the shrinkage problem?" Rich couldn't imagine that.

"No." Walter hesitated. "I'm not sure where I heard it."

No, you just don't want to tell me, Rich thought.

"Oh, for crying out loud, Walter, who'd you hear it from?" Rich asked.

"Actually, from George Nader in quality." Walter paused. "He's very concerned about the lack of control we seem to have over our inventory."

"George is more concerned over how the quality department is going to survive as his little kingdom. Come on, Walter. I'm sending you an update every week on the team stuff. Give me a break. The man is furious because he's about to lose some of his imaginary power. He's holding up shipments left and right. And, if he's so concerned about our shrinkage problems, why hasn't he come and talked to me?"

"I don't know, Rich. All I know is that the DC where your office is located has the highest shrinkage rate in the company. It concerns me. And I want to make sure you're on top of it."

"Bob and I are on top of it, Walter. If we need help, I'll let you know."

Fires were springing up faster than Rich could put them out. "At any rate,

I'd appreciate your referring George back to me if he calls again to chat. I'll do whatever it takes, but I can't go one hundred percent here and worry about the knife sticking out of my back. Donald told me to fix it."

"I know, Rich, I know," Walter said.

"Well, if you can find somebody to fix it without making anyone mad, you let me know because I want to meet them. As soon as I know something on the shrinkage, I'll let you know."

"One more thing, Rich. We really need to do something about that DC in Miami. I know several third-party guys that say they can work with us a lot cheaper." Walter's voice went up in pitch a bit and started to take on a faint hint of a whine.

Rich thought about hitting the disconnect button on the phone. "Hate that, Walter, can't imagine what happened," he'd say when Walter called back. Wouldn't it be great if you could hit a button and shock the guy on the other end of the line? You could shorten your annoying phone calls significantly.

"We'd need to have them come in for a meeting, Walter. Unless they really understand our needs, the cost comparison is worthless." The guy on the radio show said you got what you paid for. Rich had been down this road with Walter before. Talk quality. Buy price. With any luck, another project would catch Walter's eye before he started renegotiating the third-party contracts.

"Will do, Rich. Got to run. I'm late for a meeting with the marketing group."

Rich reminded himself to be thankful for small blessings as he hung up the phone. The conversation could easily have lasted thirty minutes.

The red light on the top of his phone blinked to its own rhythm. He picked up the phone and accessed his voice mail.

"Rich, this is Denise. I think we've hit the wall on this little program that we talked about writing for the field reps in the Whitehead Team meeting. Sorry, we gave it our best shot."

Rich's call caught Denise as she walked out the door to a meeting.

"So, what's the glitch, Denise?" Rich asked.

"It's hard to explain in layman's terms," Denise replied.

Rich got so tired of this attitude. He wanted to say, "Just try, maybe some term will strike a chord in my brain like the lightning did Frankenstein." Instead he said, "So try me. You never know."

"There's just no way to modify the field in the database to pull the information they want. Not without months of work. I don't have months. Do you want your new total operations system or some little program for the sales guys?" Denise asked.

"I thought I wanted them both," Rich answered.

"No can do." Denise came right back.

"Israel wasn't any help?"

"He had a couple of ideas. Nothing that was really worth pursuing. Besides, Rachel can never seem to give him up. Gotta run. Talk to you later."

Rich looked at the phone receiver in his hand. He thought they'd settled that in the Whitehead Team meeting. What in the hell was going on with Rachel?

No one answered at Rachel's extension. Rich settled for leaving a voice mail message. On some days voice mail was a Godsend, other days it was like kissing your sister. Today it definitely had a kissing-your-sister overtone to it.

Bob tapped on the door as Rich replaced the receiver. Rich motioned him in, and Bob closed the door behind him.

"I think I've got something on the disappearing lingerie." He pushed several pink and yellow slips across the desk, packing slips and invoices.

"Sounds like one of those old Hardy Boys books, *The Case of the Disappearing Lingerie.*"

"Ha, Ha. I hear they're looking for headliners down at the comedy club." Bob pointed to the pink and yellow sheets that Rich held in his hand. "It looks like those orders have three people in common. A woman named Rose in order entry, a guy by the name of Reston on Mike's crew in the dock area, and—here's the kicker—every one of these orders was processed while our new head of security was on the job."

"You mean since he came?" Rich felt the kink coming back to his neck.

"Not only that, Rich, but while he was actually working the security detail," Bob said.

"So what you're telling me is that it's time to call Leonard." Rich rubbed his neck.

"Oh, yeah, and how. I've already called him. He's going to come by for a 'routine' inspection later this afternoon. You got a few minutes to talk with us?"

"I'll make a few minutes. I just got off the phone with Walter. He's on the warpath."

"Great. Leonard and I should be done somewhere around four."

When Rich finally got to talk with Rachel, she sounded a bit perturbed.

"Look, Rich, I know you want us to help out. But I really need Israel on the phones. Besides, from what he tells me, every time he tried to talk to Denise about it, she just stalled. Israel has got better things to do than follow around behind some teckkie begging them to let him help them on their project. We've still got a department to run." Rachel snapped the words out.

"All I know is that it's got to be done. If Denise isn't willing to work on it, do you think that Israel could do it by himself?" Rich tried to keep an even tone.

"You'll have to ask him that, Rich. And until I get some help, he'll have to work after hours." The luster of Rachel's enthusiasm for redesign had definitely dimmed.

Rich called Denise back. This was starting to feel like a game of hot potato. Nobody wanted the project to end up in their hands. It sure was easier to do these teaming things on paper. On paper, people cooperated.

Denise spoke slowly and enunciated her words as if she were speaking a foreign language to Rich. "I don't have time."

"And that's your final word?"

"My final four words, actually," Denise responded.

"My final four are—not a problem, thanks." Rich hung up the phone.

Rich stopped by Israel's office. "So do you think you can handle the program we talked about in IT on your own? It looks like the IT people are snowed under."

"Sure," Israel hesitated. "I mean, I think so. Every time I talk to Denise about it, she seems to think it's really complex, but I was talking with a college buddy of mine and he thinks the same as me. Should be pretty easy."

It amazed Rich how much technical knowledge the younger employees had. But then, he thought there probably wasn't a seven-year-old in the country that couldn't beat him at any video game ever invented.

"Well, try it," Rich said. "If you are able to do a breakthrough program, maybe IT will perk up. We need to make something happen."

• • • • • • • • •

At the next Leadership Team meeting, Rachel and Bob reported on their benchmarking. They discussed the two companies they'd visited. As Bob talked about the quality process at Regency, a lingerie manufacturer who focused solely on women's apparel, George began to frown.

"Regency doesn't have a formal quality process at the end of their order cycle," Bob said. "Instead, they certify all their vendors on certain quality standards. Basically, the DC manager said they don't believe you can inspect quality into an order, it's got to be there to begin with. Their quality starts with vendors and ends with the pickers in the DC. The pickers are responsible for accuracy in the warehouse."

When Bob paused, Irving said, "That makes good sense. Why can't we back up quality to our vendors? If we're going for zero defects anyway, it has to start on their end."

"That's not going to work." George shook his head.

"It's working at Regency," Rachel said. "They have one of the highest customer satisfaction ratings in the industry. And they're gaining market share all the time."

"Rachel's right," Irving said. "Suppose that you took the people working in quality, moved them to vendor quality, each working with one of our suppliers." Several heads around the table nodded in agreement with Irving.

"What are you going to do with some of the people on the line? Are they going to lose their jobs?" George asked.

Irving hesitated. "Well, how many people are we talking about?"

"I imagine somewhere between fifteen and twenty, in this facility alone," George said.

Valerie spoke up. "I think it's more like ten to twelve."

"I'm not so sure about that," George countered. "But that is only in this facility. I've got plenty more in the other DCs."

Valerie tapped her pad with the end of a pen. "Really, George, I'm certain, it's no more than twelve here in Charlotte."

"I'm needing more guys. Especially if we're going to keep catering to everything these marketing types can think up," Bob said. "Bad enough with our own. Wait until we team our marketing guys with the customer's marketing guys. Nandy Gamble's harebrained schemes will sound on-target."

Rich tried to steer the conversation's focus. "I think Valerie's right, George. We're definitely shifting our workload. If some of the people work with vendors and some move over, we can probably use everyone somewhere else."

"I don't know." George refused to give up.

"Oh, come on George—people quit, people retire. I've got two guys right now that are getting ready to start their own mobile power-wash business. One more week and they're out of here." Bob draped his hands across his belly and dared George to refute him.

"Fine, but I'm telling you, and I'll tell upper management, I think this is a mistake," George said.

"George, I'll be happy to talk with you and 'upper management' about this. If you've got a minute after we're done, I'll try to arrange a conference call." Rich called George's bluff.

"Okay." George looked away from Rich's steady gaze. It's tough to bluff when you're not playing with a full deck, Rich thought.

"And we need to make this an action item. We need a one-page plan to make it happen. Rachel, since you and Bob observed the process first-hand, why don't you two get with George and get that done?"

Rachel sighed. "Sure, I think I have some open time this Thursday between one and three a.m."

George was the only member of the Leadership Team that didn't smile at Rachel's remark.

Rachel continued. "I'm going to tell the rest of what we saw only if you promise to give the action items to someone else."

Rachel smiled, but there was a set to her mouth that made Rich know the comment was of the "oft times the truth is said in jest" variety. He needed to ask Valerie and Bob if either of them knew why Rachel was suddenly so tense. Okay, aside from the fact that order fulfillment was at seventy-two percent, they were doing a process redesign, and she was a couple of people short. A couple of people short, that was a thought.

"Speaking of time crunch," Rich said, "Rachel, why don't you look at the possibility that some of George's people could come on board in your area?"

"That's a great idea," Valerie said. "I was just thinking that George has a couple of people that would do well on the phone with a little training."

"So, do we want to put the cart ahead of the horse and have Valerie look at the capabilities of George's group?" Irving asked. "You know, in anticipation of possible changes."

"Well, it certainly can't hurt," Rich said, as Valerie made a note on her legal pad. "Back to the subject at hand, what else did you see at Regency, Rachel?"

"Bob can probably speak to this a little better, but the computer system seemed to take care of all the scheduling. The customer service reps knew the level of inventory in real-time as well as what was en route, right down to the size and colors," Rachel said. "They have information at the start of the business day that reflects what the overseas operations did during the night, which of course, is the overseas' business day. In turn, they transmit information back to the overseas operations at the end of the US business day, which means that the overseas personnel arrive to start their day with up-to-date information."

"The information they get from their overseas people lets them crossdock a lot of the overseas stuff and send it right on to their customers," Bob said.

"What about labels and stuff?" Irving asked.

"That goes back to what I was telling you about their quality people," Bob said. "They've got quality people helping their overseas vendors get their shipments up to speed for the end customer. All the tagging and special stuff is done before the product hits the US DC's dock. Then they can stop shipments in the docking area, crossdock them with US product and send them right on to the customer."

"The DC manager said they've cut a week off their delivery time," Rachel added. "Imagine what that would do for our customer satisfaction."

"Okay, but quality isn't the only reason that we aren't crossdocking our shipments." George refused for his area to bear the whole burden of stunted distribution patterns.

"Hey, I didn't say it was. One thing—we'd have to shift some of our product. Free up more space around the dock area," Bob said.

"That's what happened at Regency. They shifted product back into the space that they had used for storage and made room for extra space in their dock area," Rachel said.

"Bob, can you get the space planning people to look at that?" Rich asked.

"Will do," Bob said. "Another thing they're doing at Regency is using their WMS to schedule cycle counting. Their system has the capability to work cycle counting into the order picking."

"How?" Irving asked.

"It schedules the cycle count right into the picker's schedule. In other words, while the guy's there on the aisle picking an item, the system's also flagged an item or two for him to cycle count," Bob answered.

"That sounds pretty good," Irving said.

"It's better than pretty good. You make the best use of your people and you know whether your inventory is accurate or not," Bob said.

"Sounds like something that Irving needs to talk to the IT people about. See if our new system can handle that. Our inventory accuracy can use all the help it can get," Rich said.

Rachel looked up. "One more thing, Regency is ISO certified."

Bob shook his head. "But we really don't need to look at that. We're making all these changes already. ISO isn't going to improve our operation, we are."

"Bob's made up his mind, but I think somebody should look into it." Rachel cut her eyes at Bob who shook his head again.

"Just pain-in-the-ass paperwork," Bob said.

George nodded vigorously in agreement.

Rich intervened. "I think you might be jumping the gun, Bob. The ISO documentation process might be just what we need to jump start the Whitehead effort."

Bob shrugged, looking as if the point was so ridiculous it wasn't worth arguing.

Rich continued. "Maybe the Quality Team charter needs to include a plan for helping get ISO off the ground."

George huffed loudly, but didn't speak.

After the meeting, Bob stayed behind. "It's not hard to tell you've made George mad."

"No, it's not. He's about as transparent as a one of those chiffon robes we make," Rich agreed. "You're not much help—I was listening to a radio program the other day—ISO might be just the thing. It would help if you wouldn't trash it in front of everyone."

"Oh come on, Rich. It's useless."

"Think about it, Bob. Suppose we don't do it because you think we need to do it. Instead, we do it because we want all these vendors with quality issues to do it. It seems to me its the same, in some ways, as Regency certifying vendors. That way we can help them get up to speed on the ISO process. We can't very well require them to do it if we haven't done it."

"Okay." Bob held up his hand. "I'm willing to give it a shot."

"So you'll encourage George to get the Quality Team rolling on that?" Rich asked.

"Sure thing, but word has it that George is going around telling everybody that he's quitting," Bob said.

"He hasn't by chance put it in writing, has he?" Rich was hopeful.

Bob laughed. "You should wish. George has been quitting since before he was even hired. Somehow he always talks himself out of it."

The time fast approached when George wouldn't get the chance.

"I wouldn't mind feeling like a rat in a maze every day when I go to work, if I thought something good was going to come out of it. You know, like some cure for industrial cancer or something. The trouble is, I think we're experimenting and we don't have a clue what is going to really happen with these changes."

— Raymond Rodriquez to his wife
getting ready for work, March

CHAPTER EIGHTEEN

Rich hunched down behind the stack of pallets on the dock. On the other side, Tony from Security Resources was having a heart-to-heart talk with the Reston guy, the one that Bob had connected with the theft of the *Slimmies* and the boxers. With the noise of the dock area, Rich could only make out a few words of the conversation. Reston didn't look happy. He said something to Tony about "my cut." No honor among thieves, Rich thought.

Dust tickled his nose. Rich rubbed it. The tickle became a full-fledged sneeze. Rich pinched his nose and willed the sneeze inward. "Pfft." He listened above the pounding of his heart for a break in the conversation. Its whispered rhythm never slowed. Rich heard the rattle of a dock door opening and any words he might have heard before were lost in the clamor of the loading process.

Leonard's firm had put a guy inside the DC to gather information on what was happening to the stock. Technically, since Bob and Rich had access to the product, they weren't even sure who Leonard had working for him. Rich knew that Bob had hired several new guys, and there were a couple of new faces in the order entry area.

He maneuvered to his left behind a taller pallet so he could straighten his back. Behind him, someone coughed. Rich turned his head and saw a fork lift driver staring at him. Rich didn't recognize the driver; he could be 'the plant' or he could be a guy wondering what in the hell the head of logistics was doing hiding behind a row of pallets. Ignoring the catch in his back, Rich straightened quickly and pretended to read the side of a carton directly in front of him.

Having sufficiently covered "This End Up," Rich turned.

"I'm constantly amazed at what you guys do – do you favor a narrow aisle configuration for the dock area?" His sentences bumped into one another in their rush to get out of his mouth.

"Couldn't say." The guy walked on by, eyeing Rich. "Can I help you with something?"

"No, I was just down here looking for Bob and noticed the carton stacking on this pallet. That started me thinking about the possibilities of narrow aisle configurations. You know how your mind will wander on you like that?"

The driver shook his head. "It's a problem, all right."

Obviously the driver thought Rich was the one with the problem. How long had the driver been standing there, Rich wondered. More importantly, was he spying on Rich as Rich was spying on the two men on the dock and if he was, was it because he was a good guy or a bad guy? And, more to the point, would he mention it to the two men on the other side of the pallet? Rich moved away from the dock area. So much for corporate espionage.

Later, talking to Bob, he said, "I'm glad Leonard put someone on the job. I think that left to me, the chances of busting these guys are slim to none."

"Yeah, well, Elliot Ness, maybe you'd better think about it. Could be there's some other places where we need to step back and let someone else handle it."

Leonard's planted employee in the DC confirmed what they suspected about Tony, the order entry clerk and the guy on the loading dock. Before security could uncover hard proof of the crimes, one of the three, Rich assumed it must be Tony, picked up on the security plant.

One day shortly after the infiltration process started, Tony didn't show up for work and the guy on the loading dock gave notice.

Bob found Rich in his office. "You'll never believe it, but the order entry clerk has a terminally ill mother. She tells her manager that she's got to go back to Kalamazoo and look after her. Leaving today, just came in to clean out her desk and get the paperwork for her check straight. Pretty convenient, huh?"

"Very. Who is Leonard sending over to replace Tony?"

"Some guy named Shammond. Guy's been with them for a few years. Leonard trusts him completely."

"I guess we can't prosecute these people?"

"No, it's the damnedest thing. You know, that 'innocent until proven guilty.' And Leonard says we just don't have enough proof. Talk with that computer queen and get her to put some checks in the system that will make it harder for people to alter the shipping and receiving information," Bob said.

"I'm ahead of you. I called her the other day and asked her to talk with the computer guy on Leonard's staff about what we could do in the new system to short circuit this kind of stuff," Rich said.

"Did you tell her that we want the machine that reaches out and slaps you on the hand when you try to alter records?" Bob said.

"No, but I should have. At least we've stopped the bleeding on this one. The good news is that Valerie's report on the quality redesign was encouraging. What did you think?" Rich said.

At the last Leadership Team meeting, Valerie had told them that all but three of George's staff had been successfully transitioned. Two had taken positions in the customer service area. Rachel reported the up side of bringing them from in-house was an awareness of Stabler and the product lines. Their training focused on the skills necessary for developing good relationships over the phone. Rachel's subdued tone didn't match her words. She'd had good people fall into her lap, yet she spoke as if she were reading the obituary page to the residents of a nursing home. It confused Rich.

Three of the other quality employees had moved over to the warehouse floor as pickers, and the other six had begun working with vendors to improve the quality of raw materials that Stabler received. The three who did not transition out of quality had chosen to leave Stabler entirely, citing "unstable working conditions" and "lack of management support." If management didn't look out for your long-term welfare, would you really think they were supporting you, Rich wondered.

"Valerie's doing a bang-up job, all right. Matching people and everything. Manuel and Mike have gotten our three up to speed in record time. You know how that goes: of the three; one's already made suggestions for improvement, one's a good worker and one is marginal." Bob shrugged his shoulders. "We'll see what happens. Valerie says that kid in customer service, you know, the geeky-looking one, well, he's really worked hard with the people Rachel got. I think that should ease some of the pressure on her. George and his team have even gotten the ISO documentation started. Sounds almost too good to be true," Bob said.

"Hey Bob, we've turned the corner."

Bob shook his head. "Rich, when Donald Stabler comes down here and tells me that Mr. Whitehead thinks we're the best thing that ever happened to his stores, then I'll get excited."

Two hours later, Barbara reported to Rich that there was an irate vendor on the phone.

"Karl Poznak with P&M Plastics. He's somewhere in between 'madder than hell' and 'in orbit.'"

P&M Plastics supplied Stabler with all their plastic apparel hangers.

"What's he got to be mad about?" Rich asked.

"Well, when I asked what it concerned, he said it concerned Stabler trying to squeeze blood out of a turnip," Barbara said. "I'm glad you're the one they're paying the big bucks to."

"Right. Put him through," Rich said to Barbara's retreating back.

About two seconds into the phone call, Rich said, "Karl, how are you doing?"

"I was doing just great. Down here in a business with profit margins the size of last year's bikinis. Then along come your quality people. Going to fix me right up. Going to show me how to make a quality plastic hanger. No, damn, I think they actually said they were going to show me how to make a world-class plastic hanger. So I let them in here with some of your engineer types and they find a short cut to one of my processes and now George is telling me that those are Stabler's savings and Stabler gets that much in price reductions. I'm glad for the help, but since when does Stabler tell me my business? I'll tell you, George, and Donald Stabler, himself, what you can do with these world-class hangers. Then George tells me if I talk to you, he'll see that I never work with Stabler again. That's world-class if I've ever heard it. World-class asshole!"

"Okay, Karl. Back up a minute. George must have been confused." Actually, the only thing George was confused on was the status of his job. "What we'd talked about was sharing savings between ourselves and our vendor partners. No one is going to force you to give us a certain price."

"No, I'm sure you wouldn't. You've got more finesse than George. If you don't get the price, we won't get the business."

"Come on, Karl. You know the breakage problems with the hanger we're using."

Rachel had been telling the Leadership Team for some time that customers were complaining about hangers breaking too easily. And the packagers in the DCs complained that they broke a lot of hangers trying to get the product on them. To go to the next quality level would mean an increase in cost that was still 'under discussion.'

Rich continued, "What we're trying to do is develop a more cost-efficient way to make a quality hanger."

"I'd like to believe that, Rich," Karl said. "And another thing, George is talking about the ISO certification. My people barely have time to get their work done now."

"Okay, tell you what. On the first issue, I'm not familiar with the project that you're speaking of. Give me a day or two to look into it. Meanwhile, you look at it and see what you think makes sense as a savings that can be passed back to us. We'll meet and decide on what's right from here on out and then let the financial guys sweat the details. On the ISO issue, we're ready to support that any way we can for you. We want the same thing for you we want for ourselves—to work smarter not harder." Rich began to scan his calendar. He'd need at least three days to get on top of the situation. "How about Thursday afternoon? Will that work for you?"

"I've got meetings all day Thursday and Friday. Forget Monday. I could do Tuesday, early afternoon," Karl said.

Rich was glad Karl had to move the meeting back. He got extra time without looking like he was dragging his feet. "Tuesday afternoon looks fine to me. I'll double check with Barbara to make sure I'm not overlooking something. She can work out the details with your secretary. We'll get this taken care of."

When Rich hung up the phone a few minutes later, he tapped his finger tips together forming a semi-circle out of his hands. The only question that remained about George's employment was when to fire him. The high hopes of a few weeks ago had disappeared into the black hole of George's resistance. George now threatened to suck everything around him into the void of his negative attitude. A walking industrial Bermuda Triangle—that was George.

Rich wondered what the other vendors had been told about the joint effort on quality. Hindsight clearly showed that each vendor should have agreed to a specific plan on how they would share the savings. Instead they would be working backwards, spending time going back and building bridges with the targeted vendors. George's heavy handedness might have cost them dearly. Actually, Karl's short fuse was a lifesaver. In all likelihood it had saved them some major headaches down the road.

Rich went in search of Valerie and explained the need for a new quality liaison. She had no good news to offer him.

"Honestly, Rich, I can't think of anyone working for George right now that would be good at that."

"Well, I don't know what we're going to do, but George has made his choice. We've got to let him go, and I'm going to need someone who can really work with these vendors."

"Let me think about it," Valerie said.

"Sure, no problem. Take all the time you want. You've got thirty minutes." Rich said as he walked out into the hallway.

At five that afternoon, when Rich sat down with George, the conversation was brief.

Once George seemed to grasp the idea that this was not a counseling session, he spoke quickly, as if he were swimming under water and afraid he might run out of air.

"That suits me fine. I've said it before and I'll say it again, you're running this business into the ground. Donald Stabler refuses to see it. I thought Walter understood, but I guess he can't override the old man's choices. I've told them all. When Stabler goes under, I guess you'll finally understand. Quality is important."

Quality done the way George wants it done is what's important, Rich thought. The time for debate had passed. Rich stood. "Thanks for the tip, George, and thanks for your time. One of the security guys will help you get your stuff to the car."

George bumped the table in his hurry to ignore Rich's outstretched hand and get out of the room.

Rich sat back down and rubbed his neck. The kink was back with a vengeance. Sometimes he wondered if Walter had a voodoo doll somewhere dressed like a logistics guy with a pin stuck through his neck.

Barbara stood in the doorway. "You look worn out. Anything I can get you before I leave?"

"You wouldn't by chance be interested in running the vendor quality program, would you?"

Barbara seemed to consider the question for a moment. "Wish I could help, but I gave up promotions for Lent. Melissa called and said to remind you about this evening's celebration. Go on home and forget this for a few hours."

Melissa had arranged for a small dinner party in celebration of Adworks sale. "Thanks for the reminder."

Kelly answered the phone when Rich called home.

"Hi, Kel. How are you doing?"

"Great, Dad. I got an 'A' on my project. Everybody thought it was so cool that I got to talk to Rita Sue Fox. And Katherine wants to know if you could get, like, Tom Cruise to endorse your underwear. She says if you do that, she'd be my partner for the next project."

"Don't hold your breath. Is your mom there?"

"No, she just called a minute ago. She's was stopping to get some black hose for tonight."

"I need you to tell her that I'll meet her at the restaurant. I don't have time to come home. I've still got a few loose ends to tie up."

"Oh, Dad, you're such a 'Wal-Mart shopper.' It's a party."

"I know, honey. Don't give me a hard time. Do me a favor, though. Take your mother to the restaurant so that she and I can drive home together."

"Okay, but don't be late," Kelly added as they said good-by.

Rich hung up the phone. Kelly had that parent/child thing mixed up.

With Barbara gone, Rich sat trying to organize his thoughts for the next day, writing himself reminder notes on the calendar. He underlined the note about P&M Plastics and then decided to go ahead and call the engineers that were working on that project. He batted two for two with voice mail. At least they would know what he wanted first thing in the morning.

Bob and Valerie appeared in the outer office. "We came by to offer moral support," Valerie said.

"Thanks. Did you get the exit paperwork taken care of?" Rich asked Valerie.

"Yes, George was a bit angry, but we got through it," Valerie said.

"I don't suppose he told you that you were running the company into the ground."

"As a matter of fact—no. But I think he mentioned that you were," Valerie said.

Rich frowned. "No doubt."

"Come on, Rich. There's nothing you could do. The man couldn't get on board. You can't coddle every prima donna that thinks his way is the only way," Bob said.

"You're right, Bob. That's why I know you won't mind if I tell you that we're starting another new streamlining of DC operations."

Valerie laughed.

"Go ahead and paint a target on your chest while you're at it," Bob said.

Rich opened his eyes wide. "Bob, I'm shocked. I thought we were getting along so well."

"Yeah, Walter Stabler used to keep me awake at night. Now I lie there worried that you and I agree on so much all of a sudden." Bob smiled.

Rich returned the smile and turned to Valerie. "So have you performed a human resource miracle and found someone to work with the vendors?"

"Walter has some spare time, I think," Valerie replied.

"Don't get me started," Rich said. Rich wondered why Donald hadn't mentioned his conversation with George. He'd have to talk with Donald and find out what was said.

"By the way, you asked me about Rachel the other day," Valerie said. "Her mother fell last week and broke her hip. They may have to put her in a nursing home."

"That's too bad. Obviously she's upset. She's sure been acting stressed," Rich said.

"I know. It doesn't help matters that her mother's in Florida. It's so hard to try and work these things out from a distance."

Before Rich could say anything, Irving knocked on the door.

"I heard about George," Irving said.

"Well, I tried." Rich sounded defensive.

"Actually, something occurred to me after I heard the news this afternoon," Irving hesitated.

"What?" Rich said, trying not to lose his cool before he heard Irving out.

"I wonder if we shipped everything in through Miami and we gave them responsibility for the MOD Act compliance, then I could do this vendor relationship thing. I mean, I think I could. I'm always working with them on their shipping, anyway. Maybe Marcus could help out some since he deals with our customers. What do you think?"

"I think from where I sit, Irving, you've got a job."

"Forget the past, it's already a part of who you are. Look to the future, it's wide open. What your career was before you signed that contract is not important now. You've celebrated those successes, you've learned from those failures. Time for something new."

— Rich Morrison to Melissa, at a dinner party celebrating the sale of AdWorks, March

CHAPTER NINETEEN

True to form, dinner that evening was a time for celebrating with a few close friends that lived in Charlotte. Melissa had called in a favor with the owner of her favorite restaurant, so the four couples had a private dining area. The kids had requested a more elegant private celebration later in the week at the Flying Burrito.

Everyone had arrived by the time Rich got there. Mark and Patty had driven in from the mountains for the evening. Of the other two couples, Laura and Phil were friends through AdWorks. Laura had been second in command for the first five years at AdWorks before she left to pursue a career in writing. Jerry and Elizabeth were friends Rich and Melissa had made through their work with Habitat for Humanity.

Rich tried to stay on track during the conversations, but several times he spaced out, thinking about Stabler's vendors and what needed to happen to bring them into a fuller partnership. Obviously they were trying to marry their vendors without having a date. And while you certainly could get a spouse by mail-order, you wouldn't have a partnership. If anything, there was already a relationship of mistrust with P&M. Karl Poznak felt Stabler had no long-term commitment.

"Rich is in the lingerie business. What do you think, Rich?" Laura's voice interrupted his thoughts.

A table of faces stared at Rich. All he could think of was plastic hangers. "Sorry, I missed the question."

"Rich is wrapped up in his work these days. We're lucky he got away for the evening." Melissa smiled at him.

"I wanted to know if we can put a man on the moon, why can't we make an underwire bra that doesn't go from-" Laura illustrated the defect with her hands. "From 'uu to vv' in six months' time?"

Reticence was not a hallmark of Laura's personality.

"Good question, Laura. Can I get back to you on that one?" Rich said.

"Hon," Phil said, "Why don't you ask the NASA engineers to solve the problem? They're the ones that sent a man to the moon."

"I could try to get them to take you in the program, Phil. Six months with the Russians in space. When did you have your last physical?" Laura said.

"I can't imagine being in one of those space stations with five other people for a week—let alone a month," Melissa said, steering the conversation away from Phil and Laura's less-than-amicable tone.

"Well, Melissa, since you can't even watch a roller coaster—let alone ride it without getting dizzy—I don't think you're a good candidate for the space program," Patty said.

"I'd miss real food too much," Mark said, popping a bite of grilled salmon into his mouth.

The group began to list everything they would miss in space and continued through the dessert course when talk turned to college tuition and why their children would ever want to wear bell bottoms.

On the way home, Melissa said, "Stop when you see an open grocery store. I want to pick up some mint chocolate chip ice cream for the kids."

A few minutes later, the ice cream mission accomplished, they headed toward the house. The street lights alternately put the Suburban into strips of darkness and light. The warm interior and the full meal could put you right to sleep, Rich thought.

Rich said, "So, was Laura right?"

"About what?" Melissa reached across the console and lightly rubbed Rich's shoulder.

"About the bras. Are the underwires really a problem?" Rich asked.

"Absolutely. Either they lose their shape or they poke through the fabric after a few months. Why?"

"No reason, except maybe I'll ask the design people about that and see what they know."

"I thought you were the distribution guy."

"I am, but if you're shipping the customer an apple, or a rotten apple for that matter, when what he wants is an orange, you've got problems."

"Or she," Melissa said.

"Or what?" Rich asked.

"What he or she wants? The customer could be a he or a she," Melissa said.

"I stand corrected. So how does it feel to be unemployed?" Rich covered Melissa's hand with his.

"Well, I'm not, yet. I still have three months of transition, but the end is in sight."

Warning buzzers sounded in Rich's head. He realized too late that he'd gotten himself into a potential baby conversation. He took his hand off Melissa's and put it back on the steering wheel. Geez, he must be tired. He didn't even want to have this conversation, and now he'd given her an opening.

"I think I've decided what I want to do next," Melissa said, keeping her hand on his arm.

Rich let out the most casual, "Oh," he could muster.

"You're really sweating this, aren't you?" Melissa said.

"What makes you say that?" Rich asked.

"I don't know, maybe it's the iron grip you've got on the steering wheel or possibly the fact you haven't breathed in the last two minutes," Melissa commented.

"That's not true. Now out with it. What are you thinking of doing?" Rich asked and would have closed his eyes while she answered except he was driving.

"I think I'm going for that Ph.D. It would work so well with the kids' schedules. If I get really bored or desperate, I could always freelance."

Rich ventured into uncharted territory. "What about that baby thing?"

"I thought a lot about it. And then I got this picture of me at fifty, waiting for a first grader to get off the bus. It was scary."

"I bet." Rich laughed. "Almost as scary as me chasing pop flys at seventy."

"You'll do that. It's just that it'll be with your grandchildren," Melissa said.

"Exactly," Rich agreed. "And grandchildren get to go home with their moms and dads."

"It's hard to believe Kelly and Andrew will be out of the house soon. It seems like yesterday that we were their age, out to change the world, but in the end, I suppose it changed us," Melissa said.

"I don't know. I started out thinking I could control everything. That things could be put right by managing them. But that's not true. It's tough to admit you don't control it all. I thought I would be the dynamic marketing man that transformed the world, and instead, I'm starting to feel like the pointy-haired guy in a Dilbert cartoon. For instance, today I had to fire George Nader."

"Who?" Melissa asked.

"George Nader, you know, the guy in quality. Long story. The gist of which is he's uncooperative on the reorganization and then he goes out and tries his best to make the vendors mad. I've been round and round with him, but he has chosen to cut off his nose to spite his face."

"Sounds like a happy time."

"I guess it's all he could do right now. Then I've got Rachel Alvarado over in customer service. She's got trouble with her mother in Florida, fell and broke her hip."

"That's awful," Melissa said.

"It is and it's making work really tough. Originally, Rachel was very excited about the Whitehead stuff, but now she's dragging her feet and getting an attitude about everything."

"That's understandable. It may be that all her points are used up."

"I don't know," Rich paused. "What points?"

"It's something I read the other day. We all have so many points that are distributed across our circle of concern: our personal lives, our careers and our social consciousness. So let's say, for example, that you have 1,000 points. For you, maybe 700 are taken with your career, 250 with your personal life and fifty with those social concerns."

"Hey, I think I've got more personal points than that. My career isn't twice my family," Rich said.

"Be honest, Rich, right now you don't." Before he could protest, Melissa added. "And that's okay, in the short-term."

Rich wondered why it was that when you tried to live a balanced life you got so stressed?

Melissa continued, "Besides, this is just an example. The point is, if you stay within that balance, whatever it is, then you are able to roll with the punches. As long as things go well in your personal life, then you are able to devote your other energy and points to work and social issues.

"Using Rachel as an example, her mother in Florida fell and had to be hospitalized. Maybe Rachel's also had car trouble, a police officer on a motorcycle with an attitude gave her a speeding ticket, her youngest child got up this morning throwing up, and her credit card bills are past due.

"She calls her husband's mother to stay with the child, arrives at work mid-morning, with her points in the red, already borrowing the energy that she usually has for work and world concerns just to get by. Then you tell her, oh, by the way, I need you to change one more thing. Whereupon she goes ballistic and you're standing there thinking, 'What did I do?' and the answer is nothing. You just asked her to use some of her points and she didn't have any left."

"So you're saying her mother falling in Florida means that she gets mad at me?"

"In a way, yes. She's overdrawn and she's resisting your request for change because she can't spend any more energy on it. She's in a conserve mode."

"What am I supposed to do?"

"Is it possible to get her some help? Eventually, the stuff will have to balance out, one way or another. So is there something that could be done to help her settle her personal life any?" Melissa listed possibilities. "Emergency child-care referrals or an elder-care case worker from the EAP. Maybe she's afraid to take time off to go deal with her mother's situation. It could be that a week off combined with some help from the EAP would work."

"I don't know." Rich raised his voice slightly.

"Is she helping you or hindering you at this point? What is it costing you for her to drag her feet and fight every move you're making?"

"Okay, okay. Uncle, uncle," Rich said. "Where's my white flag?"

Melissa pinched his arm. "Never ask for advice unless you're willing to hear it," she said. "Remember, how you approach the subject is important," Melissa paused. "You need to let her know that you're aware of the strain. That you're open to her suggestions. Of course, the only way we really deal with grief is to acknowledge and go through it. Rachel's challenge is not the pain of change in her life, it's what she's going to do with it. How she handles it. You know the old, 'When life gives you lemons, make lemonade.'"

"Okay." Rich agreed.

"I wouldn't advise you to tell her that just yet. She'd likely tell you what you could do with your lemons," Melissa said.

Rich pulled into the driveway. "Hey, give me some credit for my people skills. I'm not completely and totally the pointy-haired guy."

"Of course you're not." Melissa kissed him on the cheek. "But every now and then, there's the briefest glimpse of those horns."

Andrew met them at the front door. "Hey, you'll never believe it. I'm going to play guard in the playoffs on Friday night."

"That's wonderful, Andrew." Melissa gave him a hug. "We brought you some mint chocolate chip. Want a bowl?" Melissa was already on her way to the kitchen with the plastic grocery bag.

"That'd be great, Mom. Thanks," Andrew said.

"What happened to Steven?"

"Bad sprain. Coach doesn't know if he's going to be able to come back at all this season."

"That's a tough break for him and the team. So did you practice at guard today?" Rich asked.

Andrew's smile faded a bit. "I did. I guess I did a pretty good job for the first time."

"Sure you did. Just relax and it'll work out, you've got good court instincts," Rich said.

Andrew squinted his eyes and frowned deeper.

"I'll try to get some time to go over plays with you before Friday. It'll be fine," Rich assured Andrew as they walked into the kitchen for the ritual glass of milk and some ice cream. "Where's Kelly?"

"She's got the phone glued to her ear upstairs," Andrew said.

Rich walked to the bottom step and shouted. No answer. He knocked on the wall.

Kelly's door opened. "What?"

"Hey, watch that tone. Your family misses you, oh royal one. Time to grace us with your presence." Rich leaned around the stairwell so he could see Kelly and wouldn't have to yell.

"Daaaddd. This is an important call." Kelly closed her eyes when she spoke.

"Pretend that Stabler has just signed Tom Cruise to model underwear," Rich said.

"Daaaddd. Please."

"Your mom picked up some mint chocolate chip for you." Rich waved his bowl where Kelly could see it in an attempt to coax her down the stairs.

"Why didn't you say so?" Kelly's robed figure disappeared.

Before Rich made it back to the kitchen, he heard her bouncing down the steps.

"Hey Rich, here's that article I told you about. Maybe you can get something else out of it," Melissa said, placing a magazine by Rich's briefcase at the end of the counter.

Kelly patted Andrew's shoulder as she walked by. "Erin says that you're going to play guard Friday night. How come you never tell me anything?"

"Kel, you haven't been off the phone long enough for me to tell you. What can you have to yak about that much anyway?" Andrew said.

"Listen, you techno-geek, you live on the web sending E-mail to all your friends. Don't talk to me about how much I yak," Kelly said.

"Enough," Rich declared. Things were normal.

Melissa winked at him from across the room as she handed Melissa a bowl of ice cream. "What would you guys miss the most if you were on the space station for six months?"

"Basketball," Andrew said.

"Jake," Kelly said.

"Picking on each other," Rich added.

"Can you imagine how big Kelly's calling card bill would be? Whoa!" Andrew scraped the last of his ice cream from the bowl.

At least we have two normal kids, Rich thought.

When he woke up at two a.m., Rich convinced himself that if he just lay there long enough, sleep would return. Quality issues and vendor partnerships floated in his thoughts, picking up speed and finally flying at such a pace through his head that he almost felt dizzy. At two forty-five, Melissa questioned whether he was sick. When he told her no, she asked if he intended to toss and turn all night. He got up and went downstairs in search of some pain reliever for his head. Leaving the kitchen, he noticed the magazine that Melissa had laid there earlier for him. At this point, it couldn't hurt—it might even help.

GOOSE CHASE

"*If you want to keep getting what you're getting, keep doing what you're doing.*"

> — *Sally Nader to her husband, George, in an argument over his dismissal from Stabler, March*

CHAPTER TWENTY

Rich picked up the magazine and began to read:

● ● ● ● ● ● ● ● ● ●

HARNESSING THE ENERGY OF CHANGE

"If you always do what you've always done, the future will look a lot like the past." — *Unknown*

This quote is true only if everything else (not just what you do) stays the same. Today, the situation is even more challenging. When the environment changes, doing what you always do will result in a future even worse than the past!

ASSUMPTIONS CAN KILL YOU

Extending this thought further, one can see a paradigm that is often an invisible portion of a company's business plan: The past is a good indicator of the future. Unfortunately, for many organizations, this is not true. In most organizations today, the future is not based upon the past but rather upon the present. This radical idea can help us reevaluate our thinking about managing change.

The traditional process of managing change indicates that we used to be at Point A and need to manage the process to get to Point B (future).

Realistically, with today's dynamic environment, if we pursue the management of change, reaching Point B will no longer be acceptable performance. Since we are basing the future on the past instead of the present, we will always be behind. In addition, change brings discontinuities that interrupt the smooth flow of a simple line. For instance, when a new technology comes to market, it makes projecting from the present impossible.

DON'T MANAGE CHANGE, USE IT

We must realize that the phrase "manage change" is inconsistent. In fact, I believe the phrase is an oxymoron. To manage means to control. In today's dynamic environment, do you believe any person has the ability to control change? None of us can control change, so any attempt to "manage" change will be futile. What we need to do is not try to manage change, but rather to understand how to harness the energy of change. To do this we must understand the science of change.

THE SCIENCE OF CHANGE

Success today is based upon our ability to harness the energy of change. Unfortunately, many resist change because it often requires pain. By resisting change, we are subconsciously resisting success. Begin understanding the science of change by understanding the relationship between change and pain.

CHANGE AND PAIN

The creation of pain to accompany change is a natural function. Pain is our body's way of telling us we are harming ourselves. In a similar way, pain is an organization's signal that it is harming itself. This organizational pain may occur in quality problems, competitiveness, customer service, turnover, etc. For your organization to prosper, you will have pain. So the challenge is not if this pain occurs, but how your organization responds. A relevant quote from W. Clement Stone provides useful insight:

"Every negative event contains within it the seed of an equal or greater benefit."

THE OPPORTUNITY IN CHANGE

The challenge is not the pain—the negative event. The challenge, and in fact the opportunity, is how we respond to this pain. We must not resist change and flee from pain. We need to find a process to harness change and eliminate pain. This process of dealing with the causes of pain is known as peak-to-peak performance, and is described later.

RESILIENCE AND CHANGE

The pain of change is affected by individual's and organizations' resilience, along with the speed of change. Resilience is an individual's or an organization's ability to absorb change; or the ability to bounce back after setbacks.

If the speed of change is less than our resilience, we are able to deal with the pain. As a result, we are able to harness the energy of change and become successful. If the speed of change is greater than our resilience, the pain of change is too much. As a result, we feel stress and disorientation. We gradually grind to a halt as we fail. Since we cannot control the speed of change, it is vital that we build up our resilience and the ability to manage our resilience capacity.

Individual resilience depends on our individual perceptions of our certainty and control levels. The higher our certainty of a change and the higher our control over a change, the less energy we need to allocate to a change.

This is why we all respond differently to change. Have you noticed that two individuals faced with same exact change will react differently? The person with low resilience, a high level of uncertainty, or perceived low control, is going to experience more pain and will resist change. The person with higher resilience and a high level of certainty or control will deal with the pain and harness the energy of change.

THE TOTAL SYSTEM

Interestingly, our personal resilience has to do with our personal lives, our careers and our social consciousness. Our personal lives often control our resilience capacity. For example, if your personal life occupies all your energy for change, you are under major stress and you have zero capacity to deal with change at work. Thus if one person has car trouble, a parking ticket, a sick child, a sore knee, a big credit card bill, and a broken garage door opener, it is not surprising that he or she resists change. This person is over capacity and resists change in an attempt to spend as little energy as possible at work.

An interesting conclusion that must be reached here is that an organization has no choice but to be interested in the total person, as resiliency comes from the person's total life. Thus, organizations concerned with their employees' total quality of life, and promoting balance, are on target to better harness the energy of change.

BUILDING YOUR CAPACITY

Many people overlook the fact that managing your resilience also involves raising your resilience capacity. Guidelines that will prove useful in managing your resilience capacity include:

1. *Raising your resilience capacity comes from both increased pain management and remedy management. Pain management is an ability that pushes us from the present to the future. Remedy management requires an understanding of the benefits that result from embracing change. This understanding provides the motivation to deal with the pain of change and wholeheartedly embrace the tasks needed to achieve growth. Remedy management pulls us from the present to the future. For prolonged change (and thus prolonged success), organizations must excel at both pain management and remedy management.*

2. *Lowering the effort needed to harness the energy of change requires an organization to deal with the perceived levels of certainty and control. Certainty results from clear expectations, no surprises and continuity of organizational purpose. Control comes from participation, involvement, appropriate empowerment, and the timeliness of the information flowing in the organization. When certainty and control are high, individuals require less effort to harness the energy of change. Thus, they are more able to handle an increased speed of change and a corresponding accelerated rate of success.*

3. *The energy to deal with change comes from having a balanced life. Just as tightrope walkers must have everything in balance before they can confidently move forward with a minimal risk of falling, so too, must individuals have a balance in their lives so that they may confidently move forward. Organizations must be interested in all aspects of a person's life since things done off the job play a major role in how successful one is on the job.*

HARNESSING THE ENERGY OF CHANGE

The need to not manage change but to harness the energy of change and to understand the reality of the science of change are important. A first step in understanding the process of harnessing the energy of change is an awareness that the thought "success breeds success" is false.

A PERSONAL CASE

Let's take my case as an example. My career can be summarized as having built a successful engineering-based consulting firm while having two major detours, one in diversification and one in real estate. I have been to the peak, to the valley, back to the peak, back to the valley, and once again to the peak. Upon arriving at the peak for the third time, I made a pledge to never again travel to the valley.

Having made this pledge, I began pursuing the science of individual and organizational peak performance. I have learned a lot, and some of what I've learned may shake your beliefs. Nevertheless, the natural order of individual and organizational life is clear: Success does not breed success.

So what is the science of peak performance? It is this science that defines the process of harnessing the energy of change. It is my hope that you are able to apply this science to stay out of your valleys. Take it from one who has been there – the peaks are a lot more fun!

ACHIEVING PEAK PERFORMANCE

As I began my understanding of peak performance, I discovered that many before me had wrestled with the issues I was trying to understand. Particularly useful were quotes from Benjamin Franklin and Winston Churchill who said, respectively, "Success has ruined many a man," and "Success is rarely final."

These quotes allowed me to understand that the natural order of life is not "success breeds success." Franklin and Churchill expressed that success is not a permanent state and is often the beginning of failure. But why does this happen? Henry Kissinger lays our groundwork with the quote, "Each success only buys an admission ticket to a more difficult problem."

SUCCESS LEADS TO MORE CHALLENGES

Let's use a metaphor of life as a series of rooms. Each of us, individually and collectively as organizations, needs an admission ticket to travel from room to room. At any given point, you and your organization may find yourselves in a room full of challenges. You work hard, you overcome these challenges and you achieve peak performance.

While you're basking in your success in the first room, you receive an admission ticket to the next room with a new set of challenges. In fact, these challenges could be major problems that will send you to a valley, instead of a peak, if not conquered. These new problems are difficult because they are different from the problems in the previous rooms. Albert Einstein referred to this when he said, "We cannot solve today's problems with the same level of thinking that created the problem in the first place."

We obtain admission to a new room because of our success, but if we think like we did in the old rooms, we will never maintain peak performance.

HOW TO TRAVEL PEAK-TO-PEAK

For individuals, understanding the natural order of life is the foundation in building peak-to-peak performance and harnessing the energy of change. To use this understanding, you must:

1. *Accept the continuously accelerated rate of change occurring in today's world.*
2. *Develop a process that allows you to continuously develop and use new ideas.*

To deal with continuous change, an organization needs to undertake the following four major organization shifts:

- *from management to leadership*
- *from individuals to teams*
- *from customer service to partnerships*
- *from traditional compensation to performance-based rewards and recognition*

You must be careful to pursue all four shifts. Any one deficiency will result in your organization's falling into a valley.

FROM MANAGEMENT TO LEADERSHIP

Traditional management is passe. What is required today is both good management and good leadership. To create the necessary balance, a shift from management to leadership is required. The three elements required to make this shift are:

1. *Moving from a traditional culture to a culture of continuous renewal. Culture is the foundation upon which organizations are built. A peak-to-peak leader will fail if the culture he/she is working in doesn't embrace peak-to-peak performance. Therefore, the first task for a leader is to shift an organization's culture from control to growth, from analysis to vision, from slow decision-making to progressive action, from optimization to peak-to-peak, from fighting change to harnessing change, and from bureaucracy to learning.*

2. *Moving from wandering priorities to focus. The most important task of a leader is defining an organization's model of success and obtaining alignment with it. The five elements of this model are vision, mission, requirements of success, guiding principles and evidence of success. An organization's focus, and thus peak-to-peak performance, will result when alignment occurs with the model of success.*

3. *Redefining work from "doing a job" to "making a difference." It is the leader's job to assure motivation within an organization so that a peak-to-peak enterprise can*

overcome obstacles along its path. Leaders define motivation by how they think, how they communicate, how they work and how they treat people.

These three changes in the way organizations work are the foundation upon which a peak-to-peak enterprise is built. Without this first shift, organizations fail because there is nothing to hold them up when they begin to fail. From here, peak-to-peak leaders must move forward and shift the organization's structure from being individually motivated to one that relies on the teaming process for success.

FROM INDIVIDUALS TO TEAMS

<u>AT&T Teams Drive Change.</u> *AT&T Global Business Communications System's business was going nowhere by 1989. Several teams were created to redesign the core processes. In their assessment phase, they found that there was no accountability or coordination between how phone systems were sold and installed. And the process from sale to installation required 16 hand-offs. Customers' willingness to repurchase was a strikingly low 53%, and profits were unacceptable.*

After nine months of assessment and planning, the teams redesigned the process. They minimized the time between sales and installation by minimizing hand-offs and improving coordination within the company. After several trials, the new process was finally installed. Profits reached record highs and customer willingness to repurchase soared to 82%.

Professionals in all areas of business agree that successful organizations are team-based. The allure of teams is irresistible.

At the same time many organizations do not achieve success with teams. So, if teams are right, why all the problems? The answer lies in the following three critical areas of teaming that must be improved to become a peak-to-peak enterprise:

1. The fad of teams vs. the reality of teams. One of the greatest challenges in creating a successful, team-based organization is overcoming all of the existing team paradigms. To move beyond the fad of teams, organizations must understand that a team is defined as a small number of people using synergy to work together for a common end. They must also understand that there are different types of teams as well as different levels of teams, each with different levels of autonomy, accountability, and responsibility. All teams are unique and must be supported by leadership to achieve their potential.

2. *Self-directed teams vs. self-managing teams. Empowerment has been widely misunderstood. The failure to understand what empowerment really means has led many people to the conclusion that team-based organizations don't work. On the contrary, the peak-to-peak enterprise will be a team-based organization that sees empowerment as the leadership process of building, developing, and increasing an organization's power to perform through the evolution of teams.*

3. *Team program vs. team process. A team program doesn't work and cannot be made to work. A peak-to-peak enterprise will follow a team-based, evolutionary process by having successful teams, and by becoming a learning organization with teams pursuing peak-to-peak performance.*

Organizations must understand that teams are not just a tool to implement, but are the essence of how we work.

FROM CUSTOMER SERVICE TO PARTNERSHIPS

For any organization to achieve true success, there must be a major shift in the relationships among the customers and suppliers. An organization must be able to make the shift from traditional customer/supplier relationships to partnerships by:

1. *Moving from lip service about customer service to a customer-driven organization. Customer service is more than handling complaints well. This is old customer service. It has little to do with satisfying the customer or being a customer-driven organization. The foundation for a customer-driven organization is leadership's commitment to customer service. From this commitment, an understanding must flow from what the customer wants followed by a process of creating peak-to-peak performance focusing on exceeding customer expectations.*

2. *Moving from a customer-driven organization to invincible service. To go beyond a customer-driven organization, an organization must understand the motives of its customer. An organization must develop customer loyalty by consistently exceeding expectations, by continuously improving customer service, by being easy to do business with, by presenting no-hassle problem resolution, and by establishing strong relationships between people.*

3. *Moving from invincible customer service to a cooperative relationship. A cooperative relationship results when organizations begin to pursue projects jointly with customers to improve performance. A cooperative relationship will evolve between the two organizations through the application of the team-based process.*

4. Moving from a cooperative relationship to a true partnership. As cooperative relationships evolve, so should their level of interaction, participation and trust. By the time you become partners with your customers, your organizations will have integrated and seamless relationships.

PERFORMANCE-BASED COMPENSATION

Once the previously mentioned shifts begin to take hold, their benefits will be dampened without a further shift in compensation practices. This is because employees will still be driven by the traditional, individual compensation system.

In many firms, decades have passed since the compensation plan was changed. Although there have been numerous studies about compensation, little has changed. Traditional compensation systems consist of a pay scale and little or no recognition. The problems with these systems include lack of fairness, credibility, accuracy, and the fact that the system is used to evaluate individuals and not teams. It limits earning power, independent of a person's ability to do a job well.

It is important to note that all the best compensation systems are customized to meet the organization's needs. No two are alike, but all should follow the same basic structure. Performance-based compensation (PBC) is a system based on rewards and recognition that creates a balance for each person's contribution and compensation.

THE POWER OF RECOGNITION

Emotional recognition. Recognition is an important portion of every leader's job. Some ways a peak-to-peak leader can provide emotional recognition include making a regular habit of saying "thank you," providing specific recognition in a real-time mode, encouraging others to recognize great performance, and expressing spontaneous and genuine excitement for exceptional performance.

Individual goal assessment. The second element in performance-based compensation is individual goal assessment. People need to know what is specifically expected of them. It is important that each person's individual goals and assessments are highly personalized, and they are done in the context of the organizational goals. These goals should always be objective, observable, and verifiable, but flexibility is important when circumstances change. A rating is the result of the appraisal of each goal. By pursuing emotional recognition and individual goal assessment, the recognition component of a plan can be done properly.

REWARDS

Base pay. Base pay should be very straightforward and transparent. In fact, there is just one question a leader must answer when designing a performance-based reward structure: Should base pay be the same for everyone doing a job, or should there be some pay steps based upon seniority? Base pay should be reviewed annually and adjusted in accordance with the market.

Pay-for-skill. Pay-for-skill is a reward and development program designed to increase a nonmanager's base pay because of an individual's demonstrated capability to perform a variety of skills. Pay-for-skill programs use a series of base pay increases reflecting increases in skill proficiency. The most significant benefit resulting from pay-for-skill is increased skill level of the work force. Additional benefits include increased work force flexibility, increased productivity, improved customer service and reduced turnover and absenteeism.

Individual bonuses. At the same time individual goals are established, the bonus-for-performance schedule should also be established. The individual bonus should be based upon the performance against individual goals.

Prior to the start of the performance period, the combination of the individual goals and the individual bonus plan should be mutually agreed upon, then signed by the supervisor and the employee to form the "contract" for the performance period. The individual bonus eliminates the problem of a built-in annuity from traditional merit pay plans. This results in a fair overall compensation plan, since individuals are paid based upon their current performance. This allows new employees who are performing at a high level to receive high bonuses. And it requires all employees to continue to perform if they are to continue receiving good bonuses.

Goalsharing. Goalsharing is a program that rewards team performance. Goalsharing is based upon an organization's total performance and not on individual performance. It is up to the Executive Team to decide which levels of employees will participate in the goalsharing program and what factors will define the bonus. Thus, the goals upon which the bonuses will be paid and how the bonuses will be distributed are among the questions the Executive Team must answer when preparing a goalsharing plan.

DIFFICULTIES IN CHANGING COMPENSATION PLANS

Shifting from a traditional compensation plan to a performance-based plan can *be challenging. This is a fundamental area which many organizations are unwilling to change. A key objective of performance-based compensation is to balance each person's contribution with his or her compensation. If this balance does not exist, there will be unhappy people who won't make their maximum contributions to the organization's performance. The balance that must be pursued, however, is not an organizational balance but an individual balance. Individuals must believe that their compensation is balanced with their contribution.*

Some key processes necessary for making the transition from traditional compensation to performance-based compensation include laying a foundation for shifting through education leadership, obtaining input on the present compensation plan, and developing an implementation and communication plan. The new performance plan should be communicated during one-on-one meetings with each employee. And a performance-based compensation plan improvement team should be established.

It is only by pursuing this process that a performance-based plan can be implemented to answer the following question for all employees: "What is in it for me?" By answering this question, organizations will fuel their continuous pursuit of peak-to-peak performance.

BOOMERANG PRINCIPLES

In order to become a successful, peak-to-peak enterprise and to truly harness the energy of change, organizations must consider these four "Boomerang Principles:"

1. What comes back is exactly what is put forth. When you throw a boomerang, you don't get some other boomerang back; you get the same one. As an organization pursues becoming a peak-to-peak enterprise, the reactions, responses, and commitment received will mirror the feelings, thoughts, and commitment you put forth. In both words and actions, your dedication to creating peak-to-peak performance will be mirrored in the words and actions of others.

2. What comes back is always more than what was put forth. A boomerang gains momentum and returns at a faster speed. As an organization pursues becoming a peak-to-peak enterprise, the synergy that evolves acts as a multiplier for the evolution of renewal progress, improvement, growth and success.

3. Results are always obtained after the investment is made. A boomerang never comes back until after it is thrown. How long it takes to return depends upon many complex factors and is very difficult to predict. The same is true with the process of becoming a peak-to-peak enterprise—it takes time.

4. Benefits will be positive only if the peak-to-peak leader knows the path. Sometimes a boomerang is thrown and comes back. Sometimes it doesn't. It takes practice to know how to throw a boomerang. The same is true for a peak-to-peak enterprise. The peak-to-peak leader needs to know how to nurture the process and overcome difficulties. To assure success, the leader must have an in-depth understanding of the peak-to-peak enterprise. Only then will peak-to-peak performance result.

CONCLUSION

Unfortunately, there is no seven-step plan to help every organization harness the energy of change.

The key to success is to take action. Starting quickly and continuing to accelerate will create a sense of momentum which pulls people into the process. This involvement is sustained by the four shifts to leadership, to teams, to partnerships, and to performance-based compensation. Add to these your organization's continuous learning, and the result will be the synergy needed to create peak-to-peak performance.

ACTION SUMMARY

● *Analyze "pain" symptoms to see what they're telling you.*
● *Balance your life to increase your personal resilience.*
● *Use the energy of changing situations to achieve new goals.*
● *When you're successful, expect new challenges.*
● *Shift from management to leadership.*
● *Support teams as the wave of the future.*
● *Strive for real partnerships with your customers.*
● *Set up a group to institute performance-based rewards.*
● *Develop benchmark and performance measures.*

Keep focused on your vision of your organizational mission.

● ● ● ● ● ● ● ● ●

Rich closed the magazine and began to make some notes.

GOOSE CHASE

"They did it in "Star Wars." Why can't we do it?"

"We could, sir, if we only had an Ewok."

— Conversation between Walter
  Stabler and Charlie Patel in
  information technology regarding
  the new WMS, April

CHAPTER TWENTY-ONE

Screaming fans filled the gym on the UNC-Charlotte campus. Red, white and blue covered every available inch of bleachers, bodies, and in some cases, even faces. Wildcat sweatshirts, Wildcat tattoos, red and blue pompoms, and red 'foam fingers' telling everyone that Wilder was #1, formed a mosaic of color in the crowd. Rarely were you lucky enough to play so close to home, so the Wilder High School fans reveled in the hometown advantage.

Rich noticed the tension on Andrew's face while the teams were doing their warm-up drills. His hands fought off the ball rather than catching it. His shots – pushed too hard from all the adrenaline – banged off the rim.

"Get into your rhythm. Don't think about the playoffs. Focus on each play as it happens, make it the best play you can." Rich had told Andrew as he dropped him off at the team bus earlier. "If you do that, then without even thinking about it, you're going to pick up on the other guy's weakness."

Last year, the Wilder team had gone home after the first round. The goal for the team this year had been to improve on that performance, maybe even to win the state championship.

At the top of the bleachers, a middle-aged man stood with a video camera, filming the scene around him. Catching Rich in the viewfinder, the videographer pulled the camera down and shouted a greeting above the noise of the crowd.

Rich waved. "Going to be a wild one."

The man nodded in agreement. "I'll be lucky if I don't end up with a video of red and blue pompoms."

Rich and Melissa sat with several other parents a few rows up from the Wildcat bench.

Two minutes into the game, Andrew threw a pass high over Jake's head and into the bleachers.

"Think, Andrew," Rich yelled. "Good passes. Make good passes."

The coach signaled for a time-out, the center caught the referee's attention and the teams ran to their benches. The players huddled around their coaches who pounded their hands together and pointed to an imaginary game plan on the floor.

The spring-loaded cheerleaders bounced through a routine, leading to more pompom waving. Many of the students in the crowd were on their feet. Rich wondered how the players could even hear their coaches above the deafening noise. The official blew his whistle and the teams headed out onto the floor. Rich noticed Jake taking an few extra seconds to talk to Andrew.

The next trip down the floor, Jake moved closer and coaxed Andrew into throwing a pass. Jake dribbled the ball and drew two of the defenders out of the lane. Then he passed it in to the center who scored on a hook shot from the right side. On the inbounds play, Jake picked off the ball and made an easy basket which tied the score. The Spartans' shot clanged off the rim the next time down the floor – their miss seemed to have a narcotic effect on Andrew. He began to move without looking like he'd had too much caffeine. He found the open man and threaded passes through the defense. On the defensive end of the floor, he anticipated passes and harassed his man when they played man-to-man. The Wildcats won easily, never returning to the disorganized play that characterized the first minutes of the ball game.

At home that night, mint chocolate chip ice cream awaited the winners of the first-round playoff game. Melissa had invited Jake's parents for a celebration. Kelly met the team bus at school and arrived home with Jake and Andrew in tow.

"The high scorer and the star point guard." Melissa clapped her hands. "Good work, guys."

"Please, Mom, I could barely fit in the car with their egos as it is," Kelly said in mock exasperation.

"Ego? My son? Never," Jake's father said with a grin, and everybody laughed.

Rich noticed that Andrew's initial laughter faded into a tight smile.

After Jake and his parents left, Kelly and Melissa went upstairs. Rich lingered over a second serving of ice cream that had melted into a puddle of green with dark specks floating in it.

"Do you know much about the Mustangs?" He asked Andrew, who nursed a similar green puddle.

"Coach says they have a great outside shooter and they like to play a box-in-one." Andrew looked back down into his ice cream bowl.

"For a guy who just had a tremendous game, you're not very happy," Rich commented.

"I'm happy. It's just that, you know, I've been scoring eight or ten points a game. Tonight I played more minutes and only scored six points."

"But what you contributed was much more important—you controlled the ball, you made good passes. I mean you had some great assists."

"Still, I'd thought playing as much as I did, I'd be in double figures." Andrew shook his head.

"What did the coach tell you?"

"He said I had a great game."

"Jake said he said a little more than that," Rich prodded.

"Yeah, well, he said it was the best game I ever played. But I still wish I'd scored more points. Jake had a career high," Andrew said.

"I know, son, I know. We all love to score points," Rich agreed. "But bottom line—what wins the game—the number of points you have, or the number of points the team has?"

"Dad."

"The contribution you made to the team tonight was as important as Jake's," Rich said.

"Suppose you had a career high tonight, but the team lost. And let's say that in order to achieve your highest scoring game, you weren't as focused on defense and missed a few stops that you might have made. Then you reached your goal, but the team would have missed reaching their goal of making it to the second round of the playoffs. Do you see the problem?"

"If I say yes, will you promise not to do that walked-five-miles-in-the-snow thing?" Andrew showed the first signs of a genuine smile.

"Hey, I don't get to count this against my monthly quota of father/son chats if I don't at least tack that on the end." Rich rinsed his ice cream bowl.

Andrew joined him at the sink before they climbed the steps to get ready for bed. It seemed to Rich that only days earlier he had held Andrew's hand to steady him on the steps, his chubby toddler legs seeing each step as a mountain. Rich went to bed with visions of points and assists in his head.

Saturday, the Wildcats lost to the Mustangs in double overtime. Once again, Andrew played the point guard, making the mistakes a freshman point guard makes and looking dejected at the end.

The coach gathered his team around. After recognizing the two seniors on the team, he spoke to the players. "We were there, guys, and we couldn't quite hold on. But you played well and you played hard. Each year we move a step closer to the goal. Over the summer, what I want you to do is take this and use it to motivate yourself to the next level. But I don't want you to stop there. I want you to take it up two more levels from that and then know that there's another level waiting up there for you. Each level gives you the right to take it higher. You can't rest where you are; you've got to bump it up a notch."

Rich knew exactly what he meant.

• • • • • • • • •

Four months later, the WMS went on-line and the Whitehead Service Team met to hear Marcus and Irving's report on the possibilities that a team might locate a permanent office in Chicago where the Whitehead stores had their corporate headquarters. Marcus and Irving thought that a successful approach would be the same one they took with the vendor program: frequent contact and team members from both companies working on joint initiatives. Dealing with issues and problems with the guy across the street that you see on a regular basis seemed to work and cut down on the I-know-you're-out-to-get-me attitude between companies.

Irving and Marcus began to pass around a sheaf of handouts. Israel and Nandy were deep in a conversation about the future of green cotton. John, Bob and Raymond were debating the issue of whether the more fashionable Stabler items could work in the context of demand flow logistics. Mike Fulton, the newest member of the team, joined in from time to time. Without missing a beat in the debate, Raymond took a sheet and handed the stack to Larry who passed them on to Denise.

She smiled a tight little smile as she handed them to Rich. She's still mad because Israel's program worked out so well, Rich thought. Israel had developed a simple data analysis program for the sales force, allowing them to input customer sales and analyze them to determine the product mix that best used the customer's floor space. Initially, three reps tried it. When the other sales reps noticed how well it worked for the three guinea pigs, then everyone wanted a laptop with the program on it. At that point, Denise stepped in with her people and modified the program to include more information and to assure compatibility with the WMS.

"Excuse me." Darla came into the room. She looked around, spotted Bob, and with short fast steps, clacked over to him. Rich noticed Barbara standing in the conference room door. This didn't look good.

Darla spoke in a hushed tone to Bob, the whole time holding her hand across her chest like she was fighting imminent cardiac arrest.

"What?" Bob said, mimicking her hand motion.

"I said –" Darla started to repeat herself.

Before she could, Bob jumped up and turned to Rich.

"The system's gone down."

"What?" Everyone asked in unison. The whole table stood as if on some prearranged signal. The group headed for the door, and only Barbara's presence and steady hands kept them from trying to fit through all together like the Keystone Cops.

"Has somebody called the support people?"

"Is there a backup for this kind of thing?"

Denise led the pack and didn't even attempt to answer the questions of those behind her, but walked, looking neither left nor right, keeping her gait just below what you could call a run. The group that strode toward the computer room looked like Olympic power walkers. At the door, Mike and Bob continued on, Bob shouted back at Rich, "I'm going down to the floor."

Two information technology employees, including Charlie Patel, the troubleshooter that Denise had assigned to the DC, huddled around a computer screen. Charlie talked into the phone he had cradled under his neck.

"I've tried that, Paula. Is your screen still frozen?"

There was a pause while Paula Orr, the troubleshooter over at the manufacturing facility, responded.

Charlie punched another key. "Okay, okay. I'm trying that now."

"What's the problem?" Denise asked, even before she made it over to the computer screen.

Charlie looked up. "It's acting like it's too full. It won't accept any of the new data."

"Dump the old," Denise said.

"That's the problem—it won't let me dump the old. Its memory is completely full," Charlie said.

"Reboot the system." Denise snapped.

"I didn't want to do that until you okayed it. We may lose some data." With each exchange, Charlie's teeth seemed to clench a little tighter, making him look like a ventriloquist without a dummy.

"I don't know about that, but if we don't reboot, we've got two operations full of people that are going to stand around and look at one another."

Denise busied herself banging keys, taking the phone from Charlie so she could talk directly to Paula. Barbara stepped into the room and told Marcus that he had a call.

Bob and Mike followed Barbara in. They both walked over to Denise. "We've got a DC full of people standing around twiddling their thumbs. Can't we do something? I mean, even if we go back to paper, at least they'd be doing something."

"Not possible, Bob," Denise said.

Rich tried to remember who said, "Planning is easy, implementing is hell."

"Well, let's say it's a programming problem. How long before it's up and running again?" Rich asked.

"The WMS guy should be calling back any minute," Charlie said. "I called him when it first went down and he said he'd get right back to me."

"I sure as hell hope 'right back' is soon," Bob said.

"Charlie, get on the phone and find out how long the WMS people think it'll be until they get back to us and how long they think we're going to be shut down," Larry said as Denise tried to change the screen.

"What if they can't tell us how long?" Charlie asked.

"I don't care if they make something up, I want an answer." Larry's rational skills had escaped him in the heat of the moment.

In a few minutes, Charlie returned from the telephone. "They're not sure. No longer than a day, they think."

"A day! A day!" Bob, Rachel and John sounded like a Greek chorus.

Larry's face turned red. "You call them back and remind them of the service clause in that agreement."

"Bummer," Nandy said, and Israel nodded in agreement.

Marcus walked back into the room. "That was my best field rep. He couldn't figure out why he wasn't getting shipping information."

"So he's not totally shut down?" Rich asked.

"I guess not," Marcus said.

"His module stands alone," Israel said, and Denise grunted in agreement. The group stood around staring at the computer screens as Denise tried her best to perform the equivalent of software CPR before she administered a shock-cart-like rebooting of the system.

The phone buzzed. An IT guy wearing a Lion King T-shirt called Rich's name and held out the receiver for him.

"I know you've got your hands full, but Walter's on the line. I tried to discourage him," Barbara sighed. "Do you want to take it?"

"Might as well. Put him through to this extension."

In a second, Walter's voice came through the receiver, "Rich, how's it going?"

"I've had better days, how about with you?" Rich decided not to give out more information than necessary.

"Super. Dad just called to congratulate me, I mean us, on the order fulfillment rate. Even before we put this system in, we'd brought it up ten percent, so he can't wait to see what will happen with this new system. I told him he was going to be amazed."

"That's true," Rich said.

"And Howie Whitehead called him yesterday and told him that our service had improved by leaps and bounds. So Donald will probably call you sometime today. By the way, have you had a chance to look over those third-party proposals?"

"Not really, Walter. But I'm not sure I understand why you're unhappy with Logistics Alternatives. Carlos is doing a super job – so good, in fact, that we've been able to use some of Irving's time in other places."

Rich had convinced Donald and Walter that it made sense to keep the Miami operation as a third-party, allowing them to deal with all the issues involving the imported product and the MOD Act. The problem was the people in Miami were making it look too easy. Because of that, Walter wanted to try to get Carlos's firm to cut their price.

"I'm not. It's just some of those proposals look really good," Walter said.

"I'll look them over, but you've got to think how much it'll cost us in the long run if we get someone who doesn't do the job at the same level that it's being done now."

"I agree one hundred percent," Walter said, in a tone that suggested he was one hundred percent clueless.

"I've only got a minute, Walter, but have you had a chance to look over the proposal to develop that new underwire material?"

"I have, Rich, but before we commit those kind of resources, I think that we should study it further," Walter said.

Rich wanted to ask Walter if he remembered the Wonderbra, but resisted. 'Analysis paralysis' should be engraved on Walter's tombstone.

"Okay, but our development time is killing us on those things. Got to run. I'll look over those bids and call you back." Rich hung up the phone.

"What did he want?" Bob asked.

"Wanted to let us know what a great job we're doing. Howie Whitehead called yesterday and congratulated Donald on our success," Rich said.

"So then this probably wouldn't be a good time to have a high-priority Whitehead order lost in computer hell?" Marcus asked.

Rich groaned. "Tell me you're kidding."

"That was one of my sales reps on the phone. He took a big order late yesterday and promised it by tomorrow," Marcus said.

"Then why isn't it in the system?" Bob asked.

"He couldn't get his laptop up so he called somebody in customer service and they checked stock for him and okayed the order, so he told the Whitehead buyer that it was on its way. This morning he tried to get the order to process again and that's when it finally hit him he might have a problem."

"Pretty boys," Bob muttered under his breath.

"Hey, if it weren't for sales reps you wouldn't have a job." Marcus stared at Bob.

Rich stepped in. "Look, this isn't solving the problem."

Mike moved closer. "I overheard what you were saying about an order for Whitehead. Why don't you get the guy to fax the order in?"

"I don't think that's going to work," Bob said.

"Down there on the floor we're no match for all this great computer stuff, but if you get the guy to fax the order in, I'll pull some of our people who were around before this other stuff and we'll get that order out of here," Mike said, obviously enjoying the chance to show up the computer. "You're always saying people are your biggest asset. You believe that bull or not?"

Marcus perked up. "Can you do that?"

Bob looked at Marcus. "Hey, the people in the DC know how to get down to the brass tacks and get the work done. Of course we can do that."

Rich grinned. Bob had gone from "I don't think so" to "Damn right" in under ten seconds.

"Marcus, after you get that guy to fax the order over here, why don't you get Valerie and Raymond to help you contact all the reps and make sure there aren't any other critical orders. If we have to, we can route some of the others to Carlos in Miami."

"Suppose the Miami DC doesn't have the full order?" Marcus asked.

"Then we'll have to ship it from two places. Better that than miss a bunch of orders," Rich said, as they walked back to where the rest of the Whitehead Service Team stood. They were gathered around the computer as if it were a piano and they were getting ready to have a sing-along.

Larry looked up as they approached. "The software people tell us we're looking at anywhere between six and eight hours."

Marcus found Raymond and Valerie and explained what calls they needed to make.

Rachel spoke up. "I'm going to get my crew to start calling customers whose orders are pending in the next two days. Let them know that we'll update the status of their order by the end of the day today."

"How are you going to do that with the system down?" Irving asked.

"We're still printing backup information since the system is new to us." Rachel grinned.

Rich couldn't believe the difference in Rachel. After they'd talked four months ago, she had decided to take two weeks off to deal with her mother's situation. Israel had stepped up, and with the new people that moved over from quality, they had gotten through. Rachel had struggled a bit, had a tough day every now and then, but who didn't? Sometimes your points are all used up.

Barbara stepped back into the room and motioned for Rich. Since Walter had already called and the computer system had already crashed, it was hard to imagine what the problem could be, Rich thought as he made his way across the room.

"Donald's pilot just called ahead and wanted to be sure I arranged lunch for him."

"What?" Rich leaned closer to Barbara.

"Donald Stabler is on his way now," Barbara said. "His ETA is twelve-thirty p.m. That's two hours away."

"Damn. Walter said he was happy, but he never mentioned a personal visit," Rich said and looked back over his shoulder at the group by the computer. Maybe if he half-closed his eyes, they would disappear along with the problem.

"Heads up," Rich announced. "Donald Stabler is on his way. He'll be here in two hours."

A collective groan issued from the group.

Rich looked at Bob. "Well, I guess you got your wish. Donald Stabler is coming to personally thank you."

"I guess that's better than personally coming to show me the door. How about we tell him all this was a planned drill?" Bob said.

"Yeah, that would work." Raymond agreed. "If this had been a real emergency, you would have been instructed what to do."

"I suggest we all get busy with what we can do to minimize disaster." Rich felt like he was on one of those fast-moving elevators and his stomach had caught up with the rest of him. When Donald walked in two hours later, the feeling still hadn't gone away.

"Rich, I came down here to tell you personally what a phenomenal program you've got going already," Donald said.

"Thank you, Donald. Actually, we think of it more as a process." Rich decided to get the bad news out of the way. "Today, we've experienced a computer glitch, but fortunately, Denise and her people are on it."

Donald's unhappiness clouded his face. "What kind of glitch?"

"Some sort of system overload," Rich said. "The good news is that we only installed the system here and at John O'Connor's plant, so this only puts our two areas on hold. The other good news is that we're using a team approach, so the setbacks this glitch could possibly produce are being minimized."

"You're getting long-winded on me, Rich. Why don't you give me the nickel tour and show me yourself?" Donald said.

Rich wondered how many of his points had been sucked up in the last three hours. He was sure he'd eaten his way through all his career points, world-problem points and was on the last of his personal points. "No problem."

The tour turned out to be a real education for Donald who still thought of logistics as 'the shipping department.' Mike and his crew barely looked up when Rich and Donald came through. Rich explained to Donald that Bob had every area organized to do routine maintenance checks while the system was down.

On the floor of the DC, Donald asked, "How do you know what you've got in here?"

"Well, sir, we cycle count. You know that's one of the features of this new WMS. It lets us know when it's best to work a count of a particular product into our picking activity."

"And that works, you think?" Donald crinkled his brow at Rich.

"Yes." Rich hesitated. "It should. We've just got to get the system back on-line."

"I can remember when I knew where everything in the warehouse was. I could tell you down to the last item how many we had. I could look at a pile of jockey shorts and tell you within three pair how many were there. Course, we counted everything then, every other day. We knew our stock. We touched our stock."

Rich didn't remind him that the number of SKUs in the warehouse had grown a zillion times since then. Not hard to keep a count when all you had to count were white boxers or white jockeys.

As they were finishing the tour, Bob greeted them. "Donald, I didn't know if Rich had mentioned our ISO 9000 efforts. That documentation process has allowed us to really evaluate our activities."

Donald stopped walking. "Is that right?"

"Yes sir. I've got to admit I was a bit skeptical at first," Bob said.

What an understatement, Rich thought.

"I had no idea that there was a preventative action section of ISO. Those analytical tools gave us the leg up we needed to fix some issues before we got into real trouble. I'm thinking that the other Stabler operations oughta be certified. You know these kind of benefits would help everybody."

"Wasn't O'Connor's facility working on that?" Donald asked.

"Yes, but you know they've had their hands full. Their personnel had to focus on other things. We got a head start because our Quality Team was able to give our documentation effort a kick in the pants."

"Sounds great to me," Donald said. "We need to get on with that Rich. Sounds like we're behind."

Bob rolled on. "And you know, Donald, it sets such a great example for our vendors to follow."

Rich tried not to stare at Bob. Who was this suck-up and what had the aliens done with Bob?

"Well, sir, since Bob is so enthusiastic about ISO certifications I think he ought to take the lead on that," Rich said and quickly changed the subject.

Donald left a few hours later, headed to the North Carolina coast. "I'm on a fishing expedition for movie studios. I've been thinking of investing in films. I'm kind of thinking that Walter may need a new line of work to really show his true capabilities."

Rich felt relieved. Maybe Donald's interest in the film industry would kill two birds with one stone; it would get rid of Walter and it would slow down the Grand Prix speed at which Donald had been making acquisitions.

The Whitehead Service Team spent what was left of the day fighting the fallout from the software fire. For four months, Rich had been a cheerleader and just when he was running low on his 'can do' attitude, the others picked it up. Larry Adams was the exception. He spent the day receiving faxes from his secretary and harping on the terms of the software contract to anyone who would listen, including Donald Stabler, who finally turned and said, "Hell, Larry, if you negotiated the damn thing, fix it. If you can't fix it, go back to Boston and get out of the way."

Larry went in search of a more sympathetic ear.

In the early evening, the system went back on-line. Rich called home to touch base with Melissa.

"Don't tell me, let me guess," she said. "You won't be home for supper?"

"What was your first clue?" Rich asked.

"Could be that it's seven-thirty and you're still at the office." Melissa sighed.

"You're a very perceptive woman," Rich said.

Melissa laughed. "Flattery will get you nowhere, but go ahead and try it anyway."

"You wouldn't believe the day we've had. You know that article on change that you showed me?" Rich said.

"Yes."

"Well, we've made it to the next room. The next room in this case looks like the funhouse at the fair."

Melissa sighed again. "Does this mean that you aren't going to hear anything I say for the next six months?"

"Honey, you know I always listen to you." Rich laughed.

"And there is a Santa Claus, but I'm not planning to try and prove it."

"I'm reforming. Continuous improvement and all that. Want to go for a moonlight stroll when I get home?" Rich said.

"At the rate you're going, it'll probably be more like a daybreak hike."

• • • • • • • • •

Irving and Marcus got to do their presentation a week later. There was some debate, but the group agreed to send their recommendation for the team on to the Leadership Team and Donald and Walter with the recommendation that a small team be sent to Chicago. That item settled, the group moved on.

"The next item is Rich's report on the new underwire development project,"

Valerie said. When Rich had brought up the issue of a longer lasting underwire, the group had thought it might work to develop it with input from Whitehead.

"I talked to Walter and he wants us to study it further," Rich said.

"Hello. 'Can you say, this is a problem?'" Nandy pushed her hair out of her eyes. "Let's just wait around for someone else to do it and then we can be second."

"Suppose we give it to—who did you say was working on it, Marcus?" Rachel asked.

"Two people in development, Zeke and Shana," Marcus said.

"Suppose we give it to Zeke and Shana as their own project," Rachel said.

"Cuuull," Nandy said.

"Bottom line—Zeke and Shana are still going to have to jump through the right hoops," Bob said.

"That's true, but look how well we've streamlined the order process," Rich said.

"Rich, we've streamlined the order process, but we're still working on that product development stuff," Bob said.

"I still don't think I have enough lead time," Raymond commented.

"Let's back up and think about this a different way," Valerie said, ignoring Raymond's comment. "What if Zeke and Shana formed their own development company and we helped underwrite the expense in order to use their underwire? Do you think Donald and Walter would go for that?"

"I don't know," Larry said. "There's a lot of space that could be fuzzy in that kind of arrangement. You'd have to have a very clear legal understanding."

"We have all those lawyers for something," Bob said.

"Do you think Zeke and Shana would go for it?" Rich asked Valerie.

"Nandy knows them better than I do." Valerie looked at Nandy.

"Zeke and Shana would think it was the best. They're both like, you know, very independent."

Israel agreed.

"Well, why don't I take the assignment of talking to them and then, of course, I'll need to run it by Donald and Walter. Then it could go from there," Rich said.

"Maybe Donald is going to stop by later this afternoon," Raymond said.

Several people glanced toward the window and a nervous laugh circled the room like the wave at a football game.

"It seems to me that if you're going to have a group like that out there, then they should really fall under the auspices of the Leadership Team. There should be a liaison from among that team's members," Valerie said, "unless you're going to involve Whitehead exclusively on that."

The group agreed that the entrepreneurial venture should fall under the Leadership Team. That project assigned, they moved on to the next item, a review by Rich.

"If we review where we are in our charter after five months, we still have to increase order fulfillment by sixteen percent, on-time delivery by five percent and monitor where we are on label and pricing requests. Where we've been is that we've increased order fulfillment by ten percent and on-time delivery by ten percent. And we've designed a streamlined procedure for promotions and ticketing for Whitehead. In the process, we've also reworked some of our manufacturing cycles to produce less product more often. As you heard from Donald, himself, the other day, Howie Whitehead thinks we're making progress."

"And what's next?"

"Implementing. In a hurry. We've got four months to finish our charter," Rich said.

"The way I see it then, we've got four months to maximize the capability of the system. How bad did we suffer last week when the system was down?" Irving asked.

"Well, we had some delays, but with Rachel's customer service people working on it, no one had any surprises in terms of orders not showing up. I'm sure some of the customers that have seen improvement in the last four months thought we were just returning to our regular ship schedule," Bob said.

"Let's hope we never see regular again," John commented. "My people have come up with more suggestions to improve these smaller runs in the last four months than they did in all of last year."

"That's the name of the game, continuous improvement," Rich said and noted that his stomach didn't even cramp at the thought.

"So I guess if I were going to be philosophical," Marcus said, adjusting his suit lapels, "I'd say that if you never feel like you've arrived, then you have."

"Exactly," Rich said, and smiled.

• • • • • • • • • •

That fall, Rich addressed the Logistics Council's annual meeting with a speech, "Objects in Mirror May Be Closer Than They Appear: Don't Let Change Run You Over."

As he sat waiting to address the group, he thought about the last year. How many lessons he had learned, how many ways he'd learned them. A year ago he could not have imagined Stabler's current logistical arrangement, from third-party providers to service teams devoted exclusively to their large clients. The face of Stabler's operations had changed dramatically. Because of his experience the last year, Rich knew that a year from now, it would be different still.

A year ago, he couldn't have imagined Melissa in her current condition, nor Andrew moving into a point guard position on the basketball team and certainly not Kelly campaigning for third-world children. He knew that a year from now, they would be different still.

The moderator introduced Rich and he began to speak:

"There is an ancient Chinese curse, 'May you achieve all your goals.' The last year brought the meaning of that home to me. Almost a year ago, I stood in one of Stabler's distribution centers with a picket group on the outside and a demoralized group of employees on the inside, and Donald Stabler, our CEO who is fond of war motifs, telling me in no uncertain terms that this was war and we were losing.

"The choice was simple, as it often is when your back is to the wall and people with powerful weapons are drawing a bead on you. You figure out how to focus those weapons onto a spot and use their power to blow open a hole in the wall at your back. There you can regroup and overcome, turn the weapons that are firing on you in another direction. Use them to your benefit. At Stabler, we needed those weapons trained on an order fulfillment system that was so bad, it would rack up charge-backs in the short-term and lose customers for us in the long-term.

"You might ask, if your back is against the wall, why not just start shooting? That's a wonderful thought, but you remember "Butch Cassidy and The Sundance Kid." It's a sure way to go down in a blaze of glory.

"So how do you began the process? And let me emphasize, it is a process. There is no easy fix.

"At Stabler, the process began for us when we shifted from individuals to teams.

"I see your eyes glazing over out there. The minute I used the word team, some of you started to count the rafters. Let's face it, the word 'team' has almost as many definitions as you have SKUs in your distribution center. A wide variety of team programs have come and gone over the last thirty years. What we discovered is these programs, such as job enrichment, participative management and quality circles, to name just a few, have very little to do with a company becoming a team-based organization. In fact, these programs drive organizations away from becoming team-based organizations. Their lack of long-term success impacts every company that decides to pursue teaming.

"We owe ourselves and those who work with us so much more than that: teaming is a process. Only when we begin to look at teams as a process, to be nourished and nurtured do we began to reap the full benefits of a teaming environment.

"The key to recognize the unique qualities of teams is to understand that teams change and evolve. They need to have a clear sense of direction, a charter, a benchmark to determine whether progress is being made or whether we've managed to throw one more 'have to' into everyone's day.

"At Stabler, the process of teaming made a substantial difference in our workforce. Not that it was perfect. As one of my DC managers phrased it, 'For twenty years we've told you not to think; now we're telling you that's what you need to do.' We've had our share of wait-and-see employees and some show-me-just-show-me-that-it-works employees. But we've also had our success stories. Take the stock picker who went home and built his own model of the DC in his woodworking shed. He created movable machines and walls so that his team could actually move walls and shelving around when they were looking at alternatives for the DC arrangement.

"While teaming is an excellent process for unleashing the power of the people in your company, it is also a demanding process. Teaming demands a shift in management. Management must move from managing to leading. This is not without some fear for most of us. Without a doubt, you never go through a day that you don't wonder if you're giving up too much control, if your checks and balances are all wrong. And without a doubt, you never go through a time that you don't learn something about yourself. If everyone in your organization isn't learning something about themselves, then the organization will never change. The organization changes because its people change and because its leadership changes. It sounds so simple. Don't underestimate resistance; it's normally high. If you think letting go is hard for you, let me assure you, it's twice as hard for the guy down on the floor. Al McQuire, former basketball coach for Marquette, said it best, "No one wins a game by how much he or she knows; you win by what your players have learned."

"I don't claim to have all the answers to your teaming issues. For instance, at Stabler, we're still struggling with how to make our compensation systems compatible with our teaming approach. That will be next year's speech.

"Teams have opened up our possibilities. Without them we wouldn't have had successful efforts in our ISO 9000 certification, our third-party relationships or crossdocking, all key steps toward world-class operations. You could say that these were three of our weapons that we used when we had our backs against the wall. None of these, ISO 9000, third-party providers or crossdocking, would have been nearly as successful without the understanding of what a true partnership involves.

"Our first attempts at partnership were met with skepticism and in some cases, anger. Our partners were underwhelmed by the shallowness of our commitment. Then it hit us. We were trying to marry our partners without ever developing a relationship, and not surprisingly, they weren't interested.

"One of our first successful teaming efforts was the ISO 9000. We had competitors who were certified and beating us to death. Meanwhile, many of our suppliers needed to find a consistent level of quality. They could go from best-in-class to last-in-class in the same shipment. Did we need to do ISO 9000? No question we did. More than that, we needed to say to our suppliers, 'we're going to do more than talk the talk, we're going to walk the walk. When you have ISO 9000 issues, we're going to be able to say, you know, here's how we dealt with that issue. This is part of our commitment to you: we will be there for your ISO 9000 process.'

"In examining what we do as a part of our ISO documentation, we discovered two areas in particular where our resources were being wasted: customs and the receiving of goods. In this particular case it was because we were trying to do something that was not one of our core competencies. This held back the competitive advantage we had in other areas. So we took those issues, customs and the receiving of goods from our overseas vendors and went looking for a partner that could handle those things for us. Before we looked at our suppliers, we were careful to establish baseline data so we would know where we were. Cost is half the battle, customer service is the other.

"Ultimately, the partnering process was about the development of a relationship. Again it was a process. We were looking for commonalties in five areas:

"Capability—Does the provider have the capability to do the job?

"Philosophy—Does the provider have within its organization the commitment to continuous improvement? And is its vision consistent with ours?

"Financial Data—Any potential partner had to be willing to share its external costs, and those costs had to be in line with our needs and objectives. We combined these costs with an internal cost analysis to supply us with the data necessary to compare our actual financial results with expected financial results.

"Costs and Service—We had to know that the provider was going to be able to give us the level of customer service that we expected for the price they quoted. We encouraged many site visits on both parts, a lot of up-front communication to lessen the number of surprises later.

"Systems and Details—Does this provider have the personnel and financial resources to do the job? Do they have cutting edge capability in the areas we are considering and are their systems compatible with ours? Are they capable of ensuring a smooth changeover in operations?

"Once we had partnerships in place and our ISO 9000 documentation in process, then our teams began to see the possibilities in many other areas, including crossdocking. Product that arrived from overseas was matched up to US products in the dock area and shipped without ever having to be stored.

"Using our new processes, what were our tangible results at Stabler? With our order fulfillment at seventy-two percent we had nowhere to go but up. We revamped our entire quality department. Instead of being the guys at the door waiting for mistakes, quality became the advocates and coaches for our own suppliers and for internal departments. They began building quality into the process rather than trying to stick it back in when everything was over.

"After a review of our baseline data, our goals were pretty straightforward: one hundred percent fill rate on the first shipment, conforming to our customers' carton labeling and pricing needs and achieving a twenty percent reduction in the cost of distribution. It took twelve months to achieve the twenty percent reduction, but our first two goals were met on time. The other piece of this equation is how we surprised our customers and began to define customer service in new ways. To be honest, they would have been happy if we'd met our goals. However, for the long-term growth of our business we need to continue to grow and excel. For example, our reps are now able to analyze inventory and help buyers determine the best configuration of their floor space. For this we updated our information technology capability, but technology should not be the only focus.

"The information technology required for developing pull-through distribution, third-party relationships and crossdocking is important, but make no mistake, people drive these processes. We could not program enough information and efficiency into a system if the heart of the people wasn't in it.

"I used to think that I could change everything on my own. Then I thought if I only worked a hundred hours a week I could do it. Then I believed I could force change on other people. You'd think that as the father of two teenagers, I'd know that wasn't going to work. I might as well have painted a target on my chest.

"Finally, after many months of hit and miss, I've figured out that people, given a clear set of expectations and wide-open possibilities, will come through. There will be resistance, there will be confusion, but you can't lose your way if you have the sense, the vision of where the company is going. That's not to say I didn't have my share of side trips. I did. And occasionally on the side trip, the scenery is lovely, but bottom line—it isn't where you're going and it costs you time and money. You learn a lesson and hopefully you don't take that side trip again.

"And as for trying to make it by working those hundred-hour weeks, that serves no purpose. If I can't have balance in my life, if I don't have other interests, other outlets, then I lose perspective that is invaluable to my success and the success of my company. That's not an original thought, but it's one that, not too long ago, you wouldn't have heard in corporate America.

"So as we look to the future, what do I see? I see increased competition. I see increased customization. I see the lines between manufacturing and warehousing becoming more and more blurred.

"So what can you do? You can join the latest goose chase or you can catch a vision – visualize a goal and put yourself on the path forward. Find within yourself the ability to move from management to leadership.

"Tap within your people the drive to move from individuals to teams. Take stock and measure success. Celebrate success, but look to the next step. Move from customer service to partnerships. Every day move forward. Every day look at the big picture. Every day know that at the end of the day, world-class is an attitude.

"Franz Kafka said, 'In a fight between you and the world, back the world.' We cannot sit still and wait for the marketplace to dictate to us. We in logistics must provide solutions to problems the marketplace hasn't even begun to think about.

"So why is it a curse to achieve all your goals? Number one, you never learn any lessons, and number two, achievement brings with it an admission to the next level where challenges are harder still. Change is a challenge, but it is ever present. How we deal with change, how we harness its energy, will determine our success."

"I can't wait to see what you'll do with the other logistics problems we're having. Welcome to the Executive Team."

— *Donald Stabler to Rich, announcing his promotion to vice president, November*

EPILOGUE

Rich sat in his Suburban at the stoplight, listening to the radio's morning news. Laura had called last night as soon as Melissa walked in from her first day of classes at the university. A small giggle overtook her as she stood in the kitchen talking on the telephone, then the giggle had developed in force until tears rolled down Melissa's face.

"Laura, I've got to get off and tell Rich. He won't believe it."

Rich stood patiently as Melissa hung up the phone, gasping for breath.

"You won't believe it. Laura found out today why Sewell & Prather changed their offer." Melissa's shoulders shook with laughter.

"Well?"

"They thought that Rita Sue Fox was getting ready to sign a big contract for Sweatade—you know—that new sports drink that I was handling."

"Why would they think that?" Rich asked.

"When Thomas ran into Rita Sue at the house, he must have decided that she was there to sign a contract. Evidently, he thought the whole thing about Kelly's report was an elaborate cover-up on our part."

Rich smiled and checked his hair in the Suburban's rearview mirror, as he thought of Thomas Sewell's surprise at learning there was no Rita Sue/Sweatade contract. Rich noticed that more gray had crept into his hair, and even now the thought of Thomas Sewell was enough to make him suck his stomach in. At least his eyes had lost their hollow look.

The Whitehead Service Team was history, but the impact of completing the charter had reverberated throughout the company. Rich and Valerie were working with all the other DCs to develop the team process. Bob sat in on the meetings to offer a testimonial while Rachel and Irving helped to facilitate new teams across the Stabler logistics network. Rich now reported to Donald directly and Walter had been moved to some sort of job involving a studio Donald had purchased in Wilmington, NC. Walter spent a lot of time on the West Coast and wore wraparound shades. Hollywood would never be the same, Rich thought.

"Our Hollywood correspondent, Hedda, brings us all the entertainment news," the radio announcer said.

"Thanks, Bill. Big surprise in Hollywood. Rita Sue Fox's publicist released a statement late last night that Rita Sue and lingerie king, Donald Stabler, were married last month in a secret ceremony. It's the third matrimonial go-round for Rita Sue, the second for the underwear magnate. How long will it last, you ask? Well, this time is already different for Rita Sue. The queen of the airwaves and the king of lingerie are expecting their first child next spring."

A horn blew behind him. Rich realized that the light had turned green and pressed the gas pedal hard. Tires screeched as he moved off from the stoplight, shaking his head at the wonder of it all.

Rich walked straight to Bob's office when he got to the DC. Valerie and Bob were discussing a personnel issue.

"What happened?" They both asked.

"Just now on the radio. Donald and Rita Sue Fox are married and expecting their first child." Rich grinned. "And I thought that the old guy couldn't surprise me."

Valerie clapped her hands. "This is great."

Bob sat staring out his window.

"Hello, Bob," Rich said and waved his hands over his head. "Are you in there?"

Bob swiveled around.

"You looked lost," Rich said. "I thought you'd get a kick out of this."

Bob ticked off his fingers one by one.

"I'll get a kick out of it later. Right now, I'm just trying to figure out if I can retire before the kid is old enough to run the company."

GOOSE CHASE

— Acknowledgements —

It continues to be an amazing journey. In 1973, the name Tompkins Associates was created to facilitate payment of a speech honorarium. In 1975, we undertook our first consulting assignment. We got great results for our clients and our reputation began. We were practical results-oriented, engineering-based consultants who really cared about our clients success. It is over 100,000 speeches and seminar attendees, over $1,000,000 in book sales and over 1,000 successful consulting projects later; now we are the family of Tompkins companies: Tompkins Associates, Inc. in the United States, Tompkins Associates of Canada Limited in Canada and Tompkins Associates International Limited in Europe, in addition to our international associates around the globe.

As we have traveled the path from a small consulting firm focused on warehousing to a major force in the consulting industry offering total operations consulting with practices in warehousing, logistics, manufacturing, organizational excellence, maintenance and quality we have had the opportunity to interact with tens of thousands of industry leaders and managers. We have learned a lot as we have worked with both the world's leading companies and for many smaller firms. We have a tremendous amount of gratitude and appreciation to the many companies that have entrusted us to help them reach new levels of operational performance.

This book is a product of the last twenty-five years of interactions, successes and challenges. It was written to give back to our profession a little of what we have learned, to bring a smile to the faces of our many friends and clients and to our future friends and clients. This book is a path forward to achieving distribution excellence. May all past Tompkins clients and all future Tompkins clients relate to the challenges faced by Rich as he pursues the 'goose chase' of today's distribution world and learn from the success Rich achieves. This book is supposed to be fun, but it is also meant to light the path before you.

JT

No book is a product of only one person. Many people at Tompkins Associates assisted on this project: Sylvia Hasinger, Tonya Loggains and Shannon Seastead offered many hours of invaluable editing assistance. Nicole Blanchard did a super job with design. Bill Christopherson, Ken Nixon and John Spain read the manuscript and made suggestions. John Brown helped with the material for the chapters on quality and Rob Haynes with the team charter. Latrelle Dechene, Hillary Geoly and Patty Godin offered suggestions for change quotes, Marlyn Brock gave us the name, Slimmies, and Bonny Harrison's editing suggestions made a stronger manuscript. Many other colleagues offered support and encouragement for which we are grateful.

BJ

Tompkins Associates, Inc. is an internationally known engineering-based consulting firm specializing in Total Operations. A leading authority in logistics, Tompkins Associates has over twenty-five years experience in moving clients from planning to implementation to success. Tompkins other areas of expertise include maintenance, manufacturing, organizational excellence, quality and warehousing.

Tompkins Associates, Inc.
2809 Millbrook Road
Raleigh, NC 27616
919-876-3667

Additional copies of *Goose Chase* may be obtained by contacting:

Tompkins Associates, Inc.
Information Services
2809 Millbrook Road
Raleigh, NC 27616
919-876-3667

Quanity discounts are available.

James A. Tompkins, Ph.D. is president and founder of Tompkins Associates, Inc., an internationally recognized consulting firm specializing in total operations. He is the author of 11 books and 300 articles in industry journals and has made over 3,000 presentations. He is a past president of the Institute of Industrial Engineers, the Materials Handling and Management Society and the College-Industry Council on Material Handling Education. He received his undergraduate, masters and Ph.D. degrees in industrial engineering from Purdue University.